BIBLICAL ARCHAEOLOGY AND HISTORY

BIBLICAL ARCHAEOLOGY and HISTORY

by
PAUL W. LAPP

THE WORLD PUBLISHING COMPANY
NEW YORK AND CLEVELAND

Published by The World Publishing Company
2231 West 110th Street, Cleveland, Ohio 44102
Published simultaneously in Canada by
Nelson, Foster & Scott Ltd.
First Printing—1969

Library of Congress Catalog Card Number: 75-80440
PRINTED IN THE UNITED STATES OF AMERICA

WORLD PUBLISHING
TIMES MIRROR

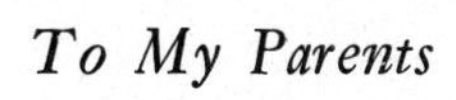
To My Parents

PREFACE

THIS book is the final result of the invitation to deliver the 1966 Haskell Lectures at Oberlin College. The four chapters correspond to the four lectures delivered between October third and sixth. The Haskell Lectures had been delivered previously in the School of Theology and then were directed primarily to a postgraduate audience. Following the withdrawal of the School of Theology, the 1966 lecture series was the first aimed at an undergraduate audience. While a very pleasant visit left me quite impressed with the maturity and depth of Oberlin students, it should be emphasized that my aim has been to communicate to undergraduates, not to converse with colleagues.

The text of the lectures was originally set down in September, 1966, when there was little time for reflection or examination of the views of others. The course of events since then—including excavation campaigns at Bab edh-Dhra‘ and Tell er-Rumeith, the Six-Day War evacuation, preparation of required excavation reports, and other writing commitments—has left little time to remedy that situation. Accordingly, the revision undertaken in the past two months has involved mainly expansion. The present text is basically the lectures read at Oberlin plus occasional illustrative or explanatory paragraphs and a few additional sections. The notes consist of minimal documentation and references to a few recent and reliable works where the reader can begin to pursue particular interests. The photographs point up some recent results of Palestinian excavations, most of them still largely unpublished.

There is some unevenness in the perspective of Chapter 3. The original text was written in Jordanian Jerusalem without firsthand knowledge of archaeological work in Israel. The Six-Day War resulted in the liberation and reunification of Jerusalem from an Israeli perspective, but to the residents of Jordanian Jerusalem it has meant occupation by a conquering power, with fear of that knock on the door at night followed by arrest and indefinite incarceration. In any case, since the war it has been possible to observe archaeological work in Israel, and Israeli colleagues have been most cordial in sharing their material and ideas. Some revisions are written from this newer perspective; elsewhere it seemed desirable to retain the prewar perspective.

I am indebted to Daniel D. Merrill and the Haskell Lectureship Committee for such a cordial reception and opportunity for a reunion with my family in Oberlin. H. Thomas Frank thoughtfully arranged all details and kindly initiated publication arrangements. Several friends have taken time to react to the lectures with constructive suggestions. I should like to take this opportunity to thank each of them, but let it suffice to mention here J. Richard Butler, Edward F. Campbell, Jr., Père Roland de Vaux, and, last but not least, my wife, Nancy. Many of the ideas in this book have been a long time in the process of formation. While it would be impossible to assess the influence and contributions of so many colleagues, teachers, and other friends, it is clear that no influence has been greater than that of my parents, to whom I dedicate this small book.

Jerusalem, Occupied Jordan PAUL W. LAPP

CONTENTS

BIBLICAL ARCHAEOLOGY AND HISTORY

CHAPTER 1

THE SOURCES OF HISTORY

FOR most people it would be difficult to propose a less exciting subject than "The Sources of History." The very mention of sources conjures up the smell of the dust on the least-used books in the library. Sources are mentioned in footnotes, and footnotes must be kept to a minimum if a book is to attract a popular audience. Not many people select a history book when they want to read an interesting story, and who picks up a historical source for leisure reading? It is a rare bird who prefers Josephus to the *New Yorker.*

For a historian, though, the mention of sources stirs emotions. Perhaps his first major encounter with sources occurred when he struggled through his doctoral dissertation. Perhaps after laborious effort he constructed a fascinating and convincing hypothesis only to discover subsequently in one of his remote sources that someone else had proposed the same idea long ago. All historians are haunted by their sources. There is always the fear of publishing a historical piece only to have a colleague point to an important source overlooked. There may even be a dread of the days and weeks and months of searching out and poring over sources in order to develop and buttress a new theory or destroy an old one.

Yet, they *are* sources. The dreary days of plodding are punctuated by new discoveries, fresh insights. The sources prove true to their name. They are sources of new ideas; without them the past would be lost and a depth dimension of life missing. They may seem an arid desert, and the historian is often wearied by the journey. At the end is an oasis, a spring, a source—refreshment for the human spirit as it presses forward on the endless path toward self-understanding. The experience of a new insight after a diligent searching of the sources excels the ordinary in much the same way as the pleasure of a drink after a strenuous trek through the desert compares with a trip to the kitchen to turn on the tap.

What are the historian's sources? They are commonly considered under two categories: literary and nonliterary. The literary sources are in turn considered primary or secondary. The primary sources comprehend all recorded data for the period: newspapers, periodicals, books, and records of all kinds—legal, political, social, cultural, economic, religious, scientific. When a historian writes an evaluation of a segment of the primary material, he produces a secondary source.

The historian who is intimately acquainted with primary sources is usually honored over one who bases his work on secondary sources. The distinction is oversimplified. In the modern period, a historian who wants to write a more comprehensive history does not have time to examine much primary material, and a fair evaluation of his work must consider how judiciously he has used secondary sources. In the ancient period, to be sure, the historian who writes a history of Rome after studying the works of his colleagues and recent predecessors deserves less respect than one who has worked critically with the Roman historians. Contrariwise, the historian who ignores the works of his colleagues and their topics of conversation will receive little respect or attention. The individual historian cannot master all the primary sources required to write the history of a broad area or period and is forced to rely on expert secondary summaries.

Nonliterary sources are frequently slighted by historians. The struggle to comprehend the literary data has often been so exhausting that little energy is left for the nonliterary material. This may be divided into two types: standing monuments and excavation results. At times these may be linked specifically with literary sources, but most often they are merely representations of the buildings, installations, arts, and artifacts of a more or less closely defined period. They add a concrete, tangible dimension to the picture emerging from literary sources. After excavation, Pompeii and Herculaneum are not just vague notions of Roman towns but the streets and statues, the homes and gardens, the frescoes and fountains of the Roman towns buried by the explosion of Vesuvius on August 24, A.D. 79.[1]

Not all sifting of the sources is as dreary as this discussion might indicate. While tracing details of the changing forms of ugly pots is a tedious part of nonliterary research in antiquity, there are compensations in artifacts of unsurpassed beauty. There are fascinating accounts of intriguing adventures to compensate for the masses of dry records. Among the many pedantic secondary sources a few are brilliant and biting. Conversely, not all the breakthroughs are as spectacular as might be hoped. Sometimes it takes years of little, apparently insignificant, discoveries to add up to a major insight. In this sense history is like other fields of research: a few major breakthroughs, more minor discoveries, and much disciplined plodding.

The disciplined examination of pertinent literary and nonliterary sources or even a brilliant idea prompted by the search is not yet history. Besides the traditional sources, there is another essential source in the creation of history: the historian himself.

There must be a fertile mind to conceive the new insight, develop the new postulation, create the new synthesis. Even ideas in a fertile mind are not yet history. They require disciplined organization and lucid presentation before they become history. Perhaps the greatest challenge to the historian comes when he has concluded that it is time to draw the line on his source examination and write history.

It may be well to pause at this point to enumerate some elements of this challenge. What are the problems facing the historian as he attempts to evaluate, synthesize, and distill his sources? First, attention will be focused on a literary source for contemporary history. This will be followed by an examination of the problems of ancient literary sources, nonliterary sources, and finally of the historian himself as a source of history. To focus attention on the problems of a contemporary literary source, we turn to an item from *Time* for August 19, 1966—an example of one of the less tedious kinds of literary sources.

Happening at the Hamptons

When the 11:01 A.M. train from Manhattan pulled into Southampton—still a semi-exclusive summer enclave on the eastern tip of Long Island—the scene that greeted the passengers was not to be believed. Rumbling and banging down the street came a wave of empty kerosene drums propelled by perfectly straight-faced adults; a horde of children were bouncing large weather balloons on their heads. In the midst of the turmoil were two homemade Hovercraft, a foot above the ground, one ridden by a curvaceous brunette billed as "Liquid Hips," the other by a menacing figure in black plastic and World War I aviator's helmet known as "The Neutron Kid."

"I think they've flipped their lids," said a bystander. The reaction from the train was stronger. "Beatniks," snorted one *grande dame* as she pushed her way toward her chauffeur-driven limousine. "It's certainly not Southampton," sniffed another. What was happening was a Happening—a combination of artists' ball, carnival, charade, and a Dadaesque version of the games some people play. The Neutron Kid, glowering through his full beard and dark glasses, was none other than Allan Kaprow, 38, the artist who seven years ago gave Happenings their name.

No Glue. For days the local newspapers had been full of the mock-solemn high jinks that Art Professor Kaprow, Sculptor Charles Frazier and CBS Producer Gordon Hyatt were concocting. The point, explained Kaprow, was to have a plan, but no rehearsal, no separation of audience and spectators. Just pick a theme, arrange the setting, and let things happen. For the Hamptons' Happening, which was to go on for three days, the theme was "Gas," in part because Kaprow & Co. intended to use a lot of helium for balloons.

Laughing gas was what it needed, decided most of the Southampton spectators. "This is a lot of nothing with no glue to hold it together," growled one cop. "Not so," Kaprow smiled benignly. "This game is dream work—the kind kids do." But he did not waste time arguing the point with critics. CBS-TV was filming the Happening, and Kaprow had to bustle his motley throng off for the next event.

Film in the Struggle. Amagansett is an artists' colony and used to anything; but even the lethargic sunbathers blinked open their eyes and squinted when a rock-'n'-roll band moved onto the beach and began blasting away in the hot afternoon sun. Then, in quick succession, giant, helium-filled balloons took off skyward, a red smoke bomb exploded, and from a plane overhead four hired sky divers plummeted downward. The doings brought crowds running from all along the beach, but Kaprow was unhappy: "I was looking for more surprises, and everything came out very orderly." It almost didn't. Two of the parachutists missed the beach by a wide margin and landed in the ocean, and suddenly it was up to the kids to paddle their air mattresses out to make the rescue.

Meantime, Sculptor Frazier was using vacuum cleaners to inflate his 50-ft.-tall "soft skyscraper," attended by scores of shoving children. "The fun is in the struggle," exhorted Art Critic Harold Rosenberg as the plastic building listed flaccidly to and fro and finally stood erect. With that, Frazier let it topple over on the beach, where, with cries of

"Kill it!", the children ripped it to shreds in a scene right out of *Lord of the Flies.*

Tons of Danger. Sunday was a day of pure surrealist chaos. In Sag Harbor, a onetime whaling port, a fake whale was seen floating in the harbor; 15 pretty nurses lay down on three hospital beds set smack in the middle of the highway. But nothing matched the pandemonium on Montauk's bluffs. There the Montauk Fire Department's hoses and two foam makers were turned loose, sending gallons upon gallons of fire-fighting foam billowing down the cliffs. Joined by hardened surfers, who left their boards to join in the fun, Kaprow, like Moses, led his tribes of happy Happeners across the foamy sea.

"There was a kind of dignity, a kind of apprehension in their approach," one spectator noted. "Yeh, sort of like a pilgrimage," another added. But soon the whole beach crowd was jumping into the cascade of suds, which came up to their knees, thighs, armpits. One plump sculptress plunked herself down, let the foam flow over her. Explained a Happener: "I'm exposing the five senses to a completely irrational environment." The suds were harmless, and they sent Kaprow into raptures. Said he: "It was like tons and tons of danger kissing you like a powder puff."

Once the fun was discovered, no one could have enough. The next day the foam-making apparatus was driven over to the town dump near Springs, another artists' outpost, where the suds spewed forth once again so that all the children could have a good wallow. "The silliest thing I ever saw," exclaimed one horrified mother. But not all agreed. "A blast—out of sight. I wish it could happen every day," said one teen-ager. It probably won't. The tab for the three-day Happening, with the cost of filming, was nearly $30,000—a fairly inflationary sum to pay for such a gas.

If you are thinking that this is a piece of fun writing with little or no importance for history, you may be right. The point is that this report is part of a vast amount of material a historian might sift through and evaluate in his preparation to write history. In focusing on this report, I hope we can see something of the character of contemporary sources and the difficulties they present to historians.

THE IMPONDERABLES OF CONTEMPORARY SOURCES

Recording

Someone who saw the Happening *wrote* a report. Perhaps the piece in *Time* was the result of several reports and several editorial revisions. Whatever the circumstances, it is important that a written report was produced. There may have been hundreds of Happenings during the week, which *Time* did not report and which were not reported at all. How many unreported Happenings have taken place recently we will never know, and the historian sifting through his material must make a judgment, really an educated guess, about how common or typical such a reported Happening was.

An acute historian is sobered by the circumstances which determine what written reports are set down for him. Perhaps this report was not filed or thrown out because it came in during a week *Time*'s editors thought there was little important national and international news. Perhaps one of *Time*'s staffers was putting in a plug for a friend. Perhaps a reporter happened to be vacationing near Southampton. Perhaps the main reason for the publication of the report was the publicity-seeking of Allan Kaprow. This in capsule form is a first imponderable facing the historian: how to evaluate the few droplets of recorded events distilled from the vast sea of unreported human affairs.

Description

The written report of the Happening is descriptive. Any event suffers from an attempt to put it down on paper, or even record it on film. Most historical descriptions are the record of what one observer saw and heard. An observer cannot see all sides or capture all nuances of an event. Even important factors can easily escape his attention. This description attempts to be more than one observer's reaction. The reporter scrambles about the Happening to see the reaction it produces here and there in his attempt to capture the flavor and character of the event. Did he succeed? Here is another imponderable facing the historian as he culls his sources. He must pass judgment on the quality of the description.

But how? If he has more than one description of the same Happening, inevitably there will be differences between or among them. He is in no position to decide which description or which portions of the various descriptions most authentically verbalize the event. He must make his decision on the basis of such considerations as the reputation and past performance of the reporter—or even the ease with which the description fits the framework in which he is viewing his material. If he has a single description, his judgment of quality is even more precarious. Perhaps there are many other elements which the reporter failed to see or which he arbitrarily disconnected from the event he described. Perhaps some of the quotations of the participants are distorted because they were ripped from their context. Perhaps the reporter heard many other remarks, the significance of which escaped him. How is the historian to know? How is the historian to decide?

Even if the report is taken at face value, the description leaves many questions for which the historian is hard put to find a satisfactory answer. Was the *grande dame*'s reaction the result of a misunderstanding, of indigestion from her breakfast coffee, of resentment linked to her beatnik grandson, or a combination of these? Was the man who thought that part of the Happening was "sort of like a pilgrimage" being sarcastic, or did he see something of deeper significance? What was the over-all reaction of Southamptonites? Who were the "motley throng"? Were they professional Happening stagers? Were they beatniks? If they were, just what are beatniks, and what characterizes these particular ones? How do they differ from hippies? What effect did the fact that the Happening was financed and recorded for television have on its character? Who instigated the children to cry, "Kill it; kill it!"? Why? These questions arise not primarily because of the brevity of the account. If the story had been longer, the list of questions could also be lengthened.

Language

The simple fact that the Happening was recorded and described involves the historian in imponderables. So also does the fact that the description is presented in language, in *words.* A regular *Time* reader would have rather specific referents for most of the words in the report, but he might stumble on a few. I presume that "Dadaesque" has a referent similar to Dadaistic, but since Dadaistic connotes to me something involving more anarchy and negation than the Happening described, perhaps "Dadaesque" is intended to refer to a more organized form of Dadaism. I was also puzzled by the teenager's interjection, "A blast—out of sight." Is this the equivalent of another expression, "A blast—gone"?

More seriously, I was not sure whether the words set down were intended to convey the conviction that the whole Happening was largely a waste of money and human resources, an expensive bit of American fun, or that there was an element of poignancy for at least some of those involved. Perhaps the reporter intended to leave this vague, but even in reports where the author intends clear communication, words frequently tend to veil rather than communicate ideas—even when people are using a common language. Here we are faced with another imponderable—the veil between the event and the historian resulting from the limitations of language and its imperfect usage.

Audience

The written description is phrased in language to communicate to a certain audience, a fourth imponderable. This piece is intended for *Time* readers, and that magazine spares no pains to identify and describe its audience—the successful, the wealthy, the powerful in business, industry, and government. *Time* fashions its writing to sell, produces reports to attract a greater audience. It is not mere fantasy to ask whether some of the details of the Happening description, or even the whole piece, were tailored to the assumption that this is the kind of thing *Time* readers want. Perhaps this is the kind of thing the *Time* audience does like to read, or thinks it does. To what extent is this Happening report just the product of the little world of *Time* and its readers? To what extent is it part of a broader trend on the American scene?

The historians of America in the late 1960's may have a hard time evaluating the significance of material from public media, such as our Happening source. They will have a limited number of individuals and groups occurring again and again in their sources. Some of these, to be sure, are influential in the events of their times, but I suspect that some of these are often in the headlines because of strong drives for publicity, fascinating or bizarre eccentricities, or because of special relations to people in the public media. For example, the only two American archaeologists working in Jordan who have been mentioned by *Time* in the last several years are far from being considered front-rank archaeologists by their colleagues; and both of these have been mentioned more than once. It seems clear that their mention is part of the small world of *Time* and its readers, for their contributions to their field have been peripheral as compared with those of many Palestinian archaeologists in this period. The imponderable facing the historian is the determination of the affective and effective audience for its sources. What audience pays attention to the report? What is the competence of the audience? What is the influence of the audience upon the report and the report upon the audience? How would Happening production experts rate the Southampton affair? Outside Southampton, who cares? What role are Happenings playing on the American scene of the late 1960's?

THE IMPONDERABLES OF ANCIENT SOURCES

So far we have focused attention on the limitations a historian encounters when he attempts to evaluate and understand a contemporary source. If the historian has problems dealing with contemporary sources, his difficulties are astronomically compounded when he turns to ancient sources, and in this book we are especially concerned with ancient history and more precisely the history of biblical times.

Recording

Even the historian who limits his concern to current political history in America faces the impossible task of comprehending many libraries of sources—the Hoover Library, the Truman Library, the Eisenhower Library, and the Kennedy Library, among others. In contrast, there is no century in Palestine's biblical period where sources would require more than one small volume. In fact, during many of these centuries we have virtually no firsthand written sources at all. This historian must be content with sporadic references to Palestine in the historical records of its neighbors and traditions about events preserved in sources dating considerably after those events.

If the number of contemporary events actually written down were compared to a few droplets in a vast sea of unrecorded human affairs, to what can we compare our ancient sources? If the historian has difficulty in determining the character and scope of an event with a wealth of contemporary sources, how is he to pass such judgment on his scraps of ancient sources? In fact, if he is to write history at all, he is virtually forced to squeeze something of significance out of every scrap. A contemporary historian inevitably sweeps aside vast quantities of material as of little relevance or significance for the history he is writing. Many ancient histories are based almost entirely on material comparable to what the modern historian casts aside. For the ancient past, the historian's construction of the sweep and direction of human events is frequently brilliant, infrequently set upon a solid foundation of sources.

Description

If we look at the ancient sources for biblical Palestine, virtually none reaches the level of description in the report of the Southampton Happening. No one in those days was out trying to get different observers' views of an event; there was much more effort spent on eliminating objectionable viewpoints. Aside from the Bible and historians of the biblical period, most of the material consists of scraps: names and titles engraved on seals or rings, bills of lading inscribed on potsherds, letters from a local military commander to his superior, legal documents related to slave trading, occasional inscriptions on ancient buildings, an inscribed stele set up by a foreign official. Sometimes it can be inferred from such material that an event of importance took place, but this is not a description of the event.

"The Bible and History" is the subject of the next chapter. Suffice it to say here that the problems of evaluating the description of a single incident in the Bible involve fantastic complexities compared with the problems of evaluating a description of a contemporary event like the Happening on the beach. The problems of literary stratification and the vagaries of the development of traditions over centuries are not present in the analysis of contemporary sources. There are efforts to excise material not in keeping with the biblical document's point of view and to denigrate anything opposed to the source's perspective. Superstitious or numinous interpretations often replace description. It is well to remember, too, that the Bible is not a very large book, and substantial portions are taken up with lists of peoples, laws, poems and songs, visions and preachments, all of which present their own distinct problems to the historical analyst.

If the historian is faced with imponderables as he analyzes contemporary descriptions, his problems are considerably multiplied when he turns to ancient sources. His material is too limited to gain any kind of a balanced perspective. Descriptions available come from a rigid perspective, are deliberately distorted, and have gone through a complex process of transmission before reaching their present form. Even worse, his perspective from living in the modern world certainly aids his judgment of contemporary sources. Such a modern perspective must be prevented from confusing the ancient context, which always remains largely a blank. His ancient sources do not permit filling much of that blank.

The New Testament accounts of the resurrected Christ illustrate the problem. If the accounts appeared on page one of the morning newspaper, our first reaction would be: I do not believe it; there must be something wrong; people do not rise from the dead. This would hardly have been the reaction of a first-century Palestinian. He is more likely to have reacted: Ah! Then he really was a messiah! We moderns might gain some feel for that reaction by studying the messianic expectations in the New Testament, the Dead Sea Scrolls, and similar sources, but are we capable of divesting ourselves of the perspectives of our modern scientific world and immersing ourselves in all the mythological, eschatological, soteriological, theological, and even political elements of such a first-century reaction?

To understand an ancient source on its own terms, from within its own world, is one of the most difficult tasks facing the historian. Because we have very little to help us reconstruct the world of Ezra or Amos or Saul or Abraham, we almost inevitably fill the gaps in the picture with something from our own modern world. Before a historian can decide what it means for his historical analysis, it is essential for him to understand something of what it meant to the people who composed and used the source. We cannot tell what a source *means* if we cannot tell what it *meant.*[2]

Language

If there are problems when the source is written in our own language, if you think you have problems in understanding and translating contemporary foreign languages, consider a few of the problems presented by ancient languages. There are many words in even the best-known languages of the ancient Near East which are simply not understood. A prestigious biblical scholar has said that an honest scholar translating the book of Job would leave his translation half blanks or dots, largely because many of its words are only traditionally understood. Job is the most aggravated case, and perhaps the statement is slightly exaggerated. Still, a large number of articles in the scholarly periodicals dealing with the ancient Near East are devoted to attempts to explain individual ancient words or to assign new meanings or nuances to them. Some of these are successful, but progress is slow. New or unknown words appear in almost every discovery of old papyri or clay tablets. The specific action or object referred to by an ancient word is often a subject of scholarly debate, and some ancient words undoubtedly refer to objects or actions unknown from archaeological evidence or in the modern world.

Even where we have a reasonable understanding of the ancient words there are difficulties. There are problems with the dimensions of words. Our color spectrum is not the ancient one. Our "blue" does not have the same dimensions as ancient "blue." Even in modern languages the lines between black, brown, and gray vary considerably. The ancient words referring to such common things as sun and rain harbor different dimensions of meaning than are obvious to us in translation. Sun and rain were not purely natural phenomena and had in varying degree a dimension of divinity or the supernatural. Even where we might least expect it, in translations of numbers, there are problems of dimension. Forty means forty, but it also may refer in a general way to a fairly large group, the precise limits of which cannot be defined.

Even more basic problems turn up when we translate combinations of words. Frequently only consonants are written in Semitic languages, and it is often possible to vocalize a word as a verb, a noun, or another part of speech. Competent scholars frequently argue over vocalizations in a given word combination. Beyond this, our modern linguistic logic and reasoning is not the same as that of the ancients. We must translate "I am king" even when the ancient language omits the verb, and the modern concept of being is entirely foreign to the ancient context. To produce polished translations, we must make periodic sentences out of a series of coordinated statements. The symmetry of ancient poetry is almost impossible to reproduce in translation. The fact that we must combine words differently means inevitably that we are restructuring ancient word and thought patterns toward a modern idiom and a modern world.

Every translation loses something of the original, and ordinarily the greater the separation in time and space the greater the loss. From their art we know that the ancients had a sense of humor, could be bitingly satirical, and could call forth common traditions and experiences by the briefest allusions. Except in rare instances all this escapes us—the humor, the sarcasm, the deadpan, the allusions, the pathos of ancient literature. These are a few of the problems arising from the language of ancient sources. It might be added that these are often compounded considerably by the fragmentary and incomplete state of the ancient text.

Audience

The audience for which ancient historical sources were intended is frequently known. The hieroglyphs on the walls in the dark corners of Egyptian temples were intended only for the gods. Many ancient documents were merely records intended for the archives in which they have been discovered by archaeologists. Something of the ritual context of many mythological and religious documents is known. The political or religious reform for which ancient traditions were re-edited is sometimes understood.

Yet, substantial imponderables remain. To what extent did these reforms merely involve the political or priestly hierarchy? To what extent did they actually spark popular movements? To what extent were orthodox mythologies part of or distinct from popular traditions? Were these traditions considered harmless stories for children, inspired religious tales, or what? To what extent are the heroes of traditions and mythologies historical persons? Had they been historically important? One often has the impression that the formers and transformers of traditions exerted considerable influence on history though they remain for the most part anonymous. It is also to be suspected that the process by which traditions were formed and developed was highly conducive to the omission and excision of many persons and events of historical significance.

We have said that the problems involved in understanding modern historical sources are at bottom our inadequacies in understanding man, in understanding ourselves. The imponderables in interpreting ancient sources are of the same kind—compounded many times. If we have difficulty understanding contemporary man, the difficulties are increased when we try to understand man living in a world remote and foreign to us. If we have difficulty understanding ourselves and our intimate associates, can we expect to understand the entirely strange patterns of thoughts and words of a people outside our experiential world? If we have insurmountable problems in understanding modern man when we have libraries full of sources and of modern scientific studies about man, what can we say about ancient man when our sources are infinitesimal?

It is something of a paradox, then, that historians frequently seem to reach more assured conclusions about the ancient world than about the modern scene. This suggests that what was considered the greatest limitation upon our understanding of modern history seems to become the key to understanding the ancient past. That is, we tend to fill in the vast gaps in our knowledge of the history of ancient man with what we know about man and the world today, or what *we* think ancient man would have thought and done. If you were to ask a mature historian to write a history of America in the Kennedy era, he might say, "It's too soon. Give me a decade or so to see the period in clearer perspective." This is tantamount to saying that the further I am removed from a historical situation, the better I can understand it.

The zenith of concern for detachment and objectivity was reached with the Encyclopedists of the eighteenth century. Today existentialist and phenomenological approaches denigrate the possibility and utility of such detached approaches to history and to life. Most contemporary thinkers would deny that it is possible to understand events of fifty or five hundred or five thousand years ago better than events of the past decade. Any serious consideration of the imponderables of history can hardly lead to anything but hearty agreement. The ambiguities and imponderables of modern history sources are compounded astronomically in relation to ancient sources. It is in the nature of the historical sources that we can never know ancient man as well as we know modern man. It is in the nature of man that many aspects of his life and history will continue to remain obscure. Any impressions to the contrary ignore the nature of man and of historical sources.

ARCHAEOLOGY AS A SOURCE OF HISTORY

It would seem, then, that ancient times are buried deeper and deeper in oblivion as time passes—except for two things. These are the advances made in the understanding of ancient sources and new archaeological discoveries. Archaeology, mostly Palestinian archaeology, will be singled out for special treatment in the following chapters, so it is fitting to pause at this point to examine archaeology's contributions to the sources of history.

Archaeology involves the study of the material remains of man's past. This begins with standing monuments but mostly deals with those elements that were buried in the ground as the centuries went by. If we went back to Southampton a few months after the Happening to look for remains of the event, this would probably be considered detective work, but if we tried fifty or five hundred years hence, it would involve archaeological excavation.

What would be there fifty years from now? More than likely nothing would be left. If there were any scraps of the skyscraper or traces of the red smoke bomb, it seems utterly impossible that anything of the character of the original Happening could be reconstructed from these archaeological remains. Only a chance epigraphic survival would preserve a real hint of the character of the Happening. Perhaps a sheet of the television script might have blown into the dark, dry recesses of a cave along the beach. Only such a find would make possible a conclusive link with the original descriptive report.

If most contemporary events leave little or no surviving archaeological evidence, what will later archaeologists be able to discover about us in the distant future? This has been a popular subject among cartoonists. One of my favorites shows two archaeologists in space suits looking over the recent excavation of three skeletons seated before a television screen, with a few empty beer cans and an ash tray, captioned, "Twentieth-century, I'd say, offhand. A religious ritual of some sort." Speculation on this subject need not delay us here, but we should take a careful look at what archaeology can contribute to our knowledge of ancient history. How important is archaeology as a historical source?

Contributions of Archaeology

First, archaeology contributes a steady stream of new written sources for the study of ancient history. Most excavations in the Near East produce some epigraphic evidence, and some unearth whole libraries and archives of ancient documents. To be sure, most of these are rather tiresome, repetitive administrative and economic texts, but even they shed some light on ancient life and traditions. Unfortunately, Palestinian digs produce fewer epigraphic finds than excavations in neighboring lands. Here important buildings are unearthed without a word of description on them. This is in striking contrast with Egypt, where the walls of important buildings are often covered with hieroglyphic texts.

Perhaps the greatest stimulus to biblical study in the past decade has been the steady stream of Dead Sea Scroll discoveries and publications. The Gnostic texts from Nag Hammadi in

Upper Egypt are providing a similar stimulus, particularly to New Testament historical studies in the 1960's. Most of these manuscripts were discovered by Bedouin or villagers, but the context of the Dead Sea Scrolls has been clarified by scientific excavation at Qumran (Pl. 18). The Nag Hammadi area calls for similar enterprise.[3]

Second, archaeology sheds light on the material cultures of antiquity. From the written sources we can learn something of the houses and palaces, temples and figurines, defenses and weapons, jewelry and clothing, cisterns and silos, pots and lamps used in biblical Palestine; but from written sources alone, even in the rare instance where a rather complete description is given, we are hard put to produce a plan of a house or a temple, a picture of a warrior or a priest in his appropriate attire, or a replica of an ancient knife or jug. Even in the rare instances of the description of the temple of Solomon in the Bible[4] or the temple envisioned in the new Temple Scroll,[5] the written sources are not clear and precise enough to preclude scholarly debate on elements of the plan. Archaeology provides the plans and pictures of the material culture of the past, which from written sources alone would remain only vaguely understood. Instead of picturing ancient buildings and artifacts in terms of our modern experience, we have before our eyes the actual buildings and artifacts used by the ancients.

A third contribution is what archaeologists call occupational history. When an archaeologist digs a heap of ruins composed of town upon town, he can describe the occupational history of the site: this site was first occupied in the later Neolithic period; after a period of abandonment, it was again occupied from the Middle Bronze age through the Iron II period; it was a very prosperous town at the beginning of the Late Bronze age; the town suffered major destructions about 1400, 1200, and 900 B.C. The occupational history of a region may be described, at least imperfectly, if there are several excavated mounds in the area, or if the archaeologist takes time to examine the surface remains of neighboring mounds. These will provide flints or potsherds which represent at least some of the periods during which the site was occupied. Topographical surveys or systematic study of the surface remains of a larger region or an entire country can produce the country's occupational history. This information about the occupational history of sites, regions, and countries can provide a valuable supplement to what we learn from written sources.

A fourth contribution of archaeology is direct elucidation of historical sources. There are times when a temple is uncovered with associated epigraphic evidence which reports who built it, when it was built, to whom it was dedicated, what some of its important festivals and rituals were, what was stored in its treasury, who its priests and prostitutes were. At such times a significant contribution is made to our sources of history. There are other times when, for example, an archaeologist comes upon a thick layer of destruction for which there is evidence wherever he digs in his mound. The artifacts point clearly to a very limited time, perhaps a quarter-century. The archaeologist knows from literary sources that a pharaoh passed this mound on a destructive campaign at precisely this time. The archaeologist is in a position to use the finds associated with the destruction to elucidate the literary source, even if his destruction produces no epigraphic finds. This use of nonepigraphic archaeological material to elucidate written sources will be illustrated and examined further in Chapter 4.

It seems fair to conclude that archaeology does make important contributions to our sources of ancient history. It contributes to the expansion of our ancient sources; it adds dimensions of material culture and occupational history often lacking in the sources. Perhaps most important of all, it helps to transform the extant sources themselves into something more concrete. It helps, in some small degree at least, to overcome the urge to fill in the ancient gaps with what we know, rather than with what the ancients thought and produced.

The Limitations of Archaeology

If we have spoken positively about archaeology's contributions to our understanding of ancient history, we must also emphasize its limitations. There is a vast chasm between the words of the most unimaginative written source and the stones of an uninscribed building, however magnificent. This chasm is traditionally defined as the distinction between prehistory and history. It is only when written documents appear that history begins. Everything an archaeologist digs up that cannot be connected somehow to written sources is either pre- or subhistorical. The imponderables associated with pre- or subhistorical material are even greater than those related to historical sources. Unfortunately, much of the archaeological material from the biblical period in Palestine cannot be directly related to texts and remains subhistorical. This means that most of the time the Palestinian archaeologist must content himself with contributions that supplement and complement written historical sources. Archaeology remains a secondary historical discipline, although at times it produces primary historical documents.

THE HISTORIAN AS A SOURCE OF HISTORY

We have examined two important factors involved in writing history—historical and archaeological sources. The third factor is the historian himself. History is written by people; to my knowledge, computers have not yet been programed to write history. The imponderables we have seen the historian confronting as he examines his sources are largely human. Why do people write down this incident and fail to record so many others? Why do people notice these elements of an event and not others? Why do people use these particular words? Why have these people written for those people? Our limitations in understanding historical sources are largely our inadequacies in understanding man. Frankly, we fail to understand ourselves—our role in society, our status in a group, our convictions in solitude. Evaluation of the sources of history is difficult not merely because mixed-up people are doing mixed-up things in a crazy, mixed-up world, but especially because mixed-up historians are part of the crazy, mixed-up world. The historian himself is his own greatest imponderable. This may be emphasized as we follow in the steps of the historian as he writes a history.

Defining the Subject

The historian must first delimit the segment of history he intends to study and put into writing. He may confine himself to a world, a continent, a state, a county, a city, a town; to politics, economics, the arts, culture, religion, society, technology, administration; to the human race, North Americans, United States Negroes, New Orleans Jews, the Irish Catholics of East Harlem; to the ancient world, the Hellenistic-Roman world, the Roman empire, Syria-Palestine in the Roman period, the economy of the Decapolis in the Augustan age, the coinage of Gerasa at the end of the Augustan age.

The precise subject is determined by the personal desires, interests, and backgrounds of the particular historian. Heredity, environment, and the times of the historian circumscribe the area within which his delimitation is made. The historian who has inherited a relatively weak mind might be able to do a creditable job on the coins of Pontius Pilate but could hardly write a history of the Roman empire. An Iranian villager who took advantage of every local educational opportunity might be able to write a history of his village or his country but could not write a history of French banks.

Less obvious are the limitations set by the times of the historian. Two hundred years ago the historian's sources for ancient history were the classical and traditional authors. Just under a hundred years ago the discipline of archaeology was born. Scientific laboratory analysis of archaeological materials is still in its infancy. Consequently, many of the highly specialized, technical topics which dominate historical research today have been possible for less than a century. The flood of new, largely undigested material tends to frighten historians from broad general studies. The predominant trend toward specialization in our times has left its mark on today's historians.

While each historian has his own limitations, modern historians delimit their topics from a vast range of possibilities. Most historians can probably describe in detail the stimulating process by which they delimited their topics, but why the process took the direction it did is another matter. Why did the historian select this particular topic? It seems obvious why an Irish Catholic of East Harlem—if there is one—writes a history of Irish Catholics of East Harlem, but is it? Perhaps it is a result of a personal struggle for self-understanding, perhaps a way to call for social justice, perhaps an easy way to an M.A. degree, perhaps a combination of these and other drives. How did this man happen to become a historian when his twin brother became a dope peddler and his sister a prostitute? What prompted him to sit in a library and write while his friends were out demonstrating, rioting, and looting? Was it a great act of courage or a base act of cowardice that kept him there—or a combination of both plus a tremendous number of additional complex factors? Answers to such questions tend to be complex and never completely satisfying. As the historian sits in his study busily writing, there is always an element of mystification about why he is writing about this particular subject at this particular time. If not, the historian has been deceived by a simplistic view of man and underestimates the imponderables of history.

Examining the Sources

After defining his subject, the historian must delimit and critically examine his sources. With an ancient source like the Bible the task of critical examination is fairly obvious. Statements about the sun standing still, sticks turning to serpents, and angels slaying armies require critical understanding. The task is not an easy one. There is no clear-cut method or set of principles by which the authentic elements in variant accounts can be determined with any kind of scholarly consensus. The task is not simple even with a modern source, as a look at the Happening source should indicate.

The historian is not like the reader of a novel. He cannot stop after he has gained a mental picture of the Happening at the Hamptons. His examination must lead to a critical understanding of the source. He must ask such questions as (1) how this event relates to other Happenings, (2) how widespread Happenings are, (3) to what extent Happenings form a trend, and (4) how such a trend is related to other trends and movements in the current American scene.

Among other things, the answer to the first question requires examination of a broad and representative selection of Happenings and a determination of what elements at Southampton were common, what were unusual. It might be suspected, for instance, that this was a staged event with more of the form than the substance of a Happening. The historian might decide to consider this source suspect as evidence on Happenings but to reconsider it as a piece of evidence on the influence of the public media on the current American scene. He might decide that it was a fairly typical Happening. He might even consider it a precedent-setting event which broke new ground or gave Happenings a new direction—or directionlessness. The answer depends on the personal judgment of the historian.

The second question calls for statistics. What are the ages and backgrounds of the participants? What portion of which elements of what American communities are involved? Are Happenings limited to certain regional areas? Are Happenings gaining or losing popularity and with what groups? All the statistical data, even if they were available, would not really tell the historian how widespread Happenings are in a very meaningful way. He needs comparative material: if 5 per cent of the population is participating in Happenings or if two out of three Americans never heard of them, he must be able to judge whether these figures are comparatively high or low in relation to related phenomena past and present. No one will debate the point that people can lie with statistics. In dealing with such data, only by dint of great effort and discrimination can the historian evade lying with statistics.

The answer to the third question requires the historian's powers of creative observation. Are Happenings isolated phenomena or part of a trend? Might certain Happenings be the products of different trends than others? If they have diverse origins, are there common elements that justify consideration of Happenings as a somewhat unified trend? Investigation might suggest that one Happening was the product of *avant-garde* drama, another a new medium of Madison Avenue promotion, another the result of a development in entertainment at high-society parties. If Happenings have such diverse origins, is it possible to consider them a single trend? If Happenings are on the increase and if they are changing, in what areas and among what groups are they becoming popular, and what are the changes? What are the directions trends are taking? No two competent historians would be likely to give even very similar answers to these questions. Such answers involve the highly personal judgment of the historian.

Such questions are simple compared with those about the relation of a Happening trend to other trends and movements in society. One observer linked the Happening with beatniks. What are the links? Are Happenings a product of the beatnik crowd, or do Happenings help to create the beatnik phenomenon? Hippies, too, are linked with Happenings. What is the relation between beatniks and hippies, and hippies and Happenings? Some hippies use hallucinogenic drugs. Is there any relation between drugged experience and Happenings? Hippies and other groups are frequently involved in protest demonstrations, and some of these are occasionally described as Happenings. What is the influence of Happenings on demonstrations and vice versa?

While satisfying and accurate assessments of these relations are hard to come by, relations between Happenings and broader complexes of trends are still more difficult to understand. To what extent are happenings a product of such trends as expanding leisure time, increasing freedom (or formlessness or lawlessness) in the arts, growing secularization of society, the rising stridence of youthful revolt against adult standards? With the last, such problems arise as whether Happenings are part of a traditional trend of youthful rebellion in American society or whether they represent a more radical disillusionment with adult standards or even those of Western society.

This last problem puts into clear focus the difficulty of distinguishing between the historian's task of critically examining and understanding his sources and the subsequent job of evaluating their significance. It might be possible to compare the characteristics of past youthful rebellion with those now present and distinguish new elements or dimensions of rebellion. The historian might then understand these new elements as an indication of more radical rebellion. "I read the evidence as supporting the view of a more radical rebellion," he might remark. But more than reading and comprehension are involved. The historian has attributed a certain significance to the new elements. According to his set of values, the new elements indicate a more radical rebellion. Another historian might read the new elements as failing to suggest more radical rebellion because he attributes a different significance to the new elements. The interactive character of critical understanding and evaluation makes the distinction difficult, but the historian who makes his evaluations without adequate understanding of the evidence is certainly culpable. Historians evaluate each other in terms of the breadth and depth of their understanding of sources, and their evaluations and conclusions are judged accordingly.

Evaluating the Sources

Critically examining and understanding the sources involves objective and subjective elements. The objective facts from certain sources are accepted by all historians, but historians often vary considerably in their understandings of the events described in their sources. Similarly, there are certain objective standards of value upon which historians agree. An eyewitness account has more value than a secondhand description. The disinterested observer is more to be trusted than the partisan. Still, the historian's set of values is ultimately and substantially a personal construction. It will be influenced undoubtedly by the evaluations of other historians and by the sources themselves, but the ultimate responsibility for deciding what is to be ignored, what stressed, what distorts, what clarifies, what is vestigial, what is prophetic rests directly upon the historian and the set of values he constructs. Beyond this, the set of values can never be applied in an entirely mechanical fashion. There is something of the subjective and personal in the evaluation of each and every source. There are certainly cases in which the secondhand source has corrected false impressions of an eyewitness and in which a partisan has been a keener observer than a disinterested reporter.

The problems of evaluation may be illustrated from our Happening source. The significance of this Happening is not something that emerges directly from comparative Happening statistics or from a clear perspective on its place in the American scene. Significance or value is something attributed to this event by the historian. Two respected historians using the same evidence might come to diametrically opposed conclusions about the significance of the Happening. One might seize on it as the epitome of an influential and precedent-setting trend in America today. Another might dismiss it as a phenomenon of the lunatic fringe. The same might apply to the entire Happening movement. One historian might consider the Happening crowd the torchbearers of the younger generation; another might dismiss them as belonging to the group of misfits and messiahs which every generation produces, whereas of significance for history is the preponderance of students who cut their hair and do their homework.

The relative value placed on other facets of history affects the historian's evaluation of their influence on Happenings. If the significance of politics is emphasized, it might be argued that Happenings were largely nurtured by the character and style of the Kennedy administration. If economics is emphasized, it might be argued that without the burgeoning of leisure time, Happenings might never have happened. The relative significance in history of political, economic, military, social, psychological, cultural, religious, and other factors in the historian's set of values inevitably colors everything he thinks and says as a historian. Is man primarily a political animal, an economic creature, or a social character? Because men are all of these in varying combinations at different times, each historian's set of values will be unique and continue to change from time to time. Each history remains an individual, personal, and timely statement. Even if the historian has not consciously articulated a set of values, these can be deduced from his work. Each history tells at least as much about its author's own set of values as about the values of history.

Composing History

It is perhaps more common to talk about historians recording history, but every historical record is a historian's composition. The composition may take on a number of forms: thematic essay, narrative, literary conversation, scientific analysis. Most ancient histories consist of a re-examination of the historical sources in conversation with colleagues who have made significant written contributions. Sometimes history is written as if the author were completely detached from his composition. At other times the historian reacts very personally to his subject.

In a recent historical work the author finds one Roman source "so engaging that one would have liked to marry him."[6] The proper historian (and too many historians are proper to prudish) is perhaps relieved to learn that this historian is a woman, but this will hardly relieve his icy disdain and revulsion toward such remarks. To me the perceptive and personal fascination of an author like Freya Stark communicates more history than the deceptively detached, dry documentation of most scholars of Roman history.

Among the greatest challenges to the historian is the selection and construction of the framework within which he will write his history. This is of course informed by his understandings and evaluations of his material, but a list of values does not provide an outline for a historical composition. The framework involves much more than putting down a composition outline. It involves the attempt to express in a clear and convincing way the understandings and evaluations wrested from the sources. Can I best communicate by focusing on great men and events or upon typical occurrences and the common man? Will my views be most cogently presented by concentration on the concrete and factual or upon the mood, spirit, and temper of the times? Answers to such questions as these have implications for the literary form selected by the historian and its framework. The framework is his personal construction, as is everything the historian puts into it. It is undoubtedly a mosaic of understandings and values gleaned from others, but, unless he is a plagiarizer, it is his personal composition in structure and content.

An interesting way to focus upon the problem of setting the historian's understandings and evaluations into a framework is to ask, in a favorite phrase of Paul Tillich's, who are the bearers of history. Tillich considered states the primary bearers of history, but he acknowledged that groups within states exercise influence and even individuals at times symbolically represent a history-bearing group.[7] Especially when facets of states are under consideration (and these are the building blocks of history), more emphasis may be given to groups and individuals who have left their mark on history. The framework of the historian might well reflect his assessment of the major bearers of his history. His composition is then focused upon the bearers of history.

THE FOUNDATIONS OF HISTORY

At the bottom of all this is a crucial foundation. It is the assumption, the conviction, the faith that a framework *can* be constructed which will aid man in understanding himself and his past.[8] Anyone who writes history affirms that he has some understanding of man past and present. Some would perhaps rather affirm that they merely understand man in certain bygone periods, but it is difficult to see how someone living completely in the past could be considered a historian. His writings could hardly communicate much to those living in the present. Historians write not for their ancestors but for their contemporaries.

This affirmation of human understanding by the historian seems to fly in the face of all that we have been saying about the sources of history. "Imponderable" implies not capable of being weighed or evaluated. We saw that many elements of current historical sources are imponderable. We saw that infinitely greater imponderables are involved when dealing with ancient sources. We saw that the imponderables involved in dealing with historical sources are, at bottom, problems of human understanding, of self-understanding. Despite this lack of self-understand ing, the historian affirms that he can understand human history. Indeed, he can construct a scheme for critically understanding human events, determine their relative significance, construct a framework which authentically presents these events, and put into words understandings of human history which will be meaningful to his contemporaries.

This belief of the historian that he can construct a historical framework and write a historical work borders on the paradoxical or the absurd. Despite all evidence to the contrary, I believe that I can write history. I do not really understand myself; I do not really understand human beings and human nature; yet, I am capable of setting down understandings of the course of human events. It is the paradox involved in saying, "Give me fifty years, and I will be able to write a history of the events of the past few years." The present is a bit too complex for me to comprehend and understand, but I am convinced that I will understand these events when I can view them from a broader perspective.

This belief, this faith involves more than paradox and the absurd. It involves man's very humanity, for one of man's most distinguishing characteristics is his ability to write, to record past events, to see himself in a historical context. The writing of history is man's assertion of his own humanity. It is his assertion that he can understand at least something of himself, his world, and his past. It is an assertion of faith, not based on a rational reflection upon the sources of history. It is usually an assertion made in a convincing way by a respected individual.

This assertive character of a historical work deserves some attention. It may be that the difficulty of producing a history of the contemporary scene is related to the fact that many strong individuals are making heterogeneous assertions about current historical developments. As one looks to the past there are fewer and fewer strong individuals making assertions about the particular historical period. If an especially competent person makes a strong and convincing case for his interpretation of that period, it carries the day and becomes an accepted interpretation. It may remain the orthodox interpretation of the period until, twenty-five or fifty years later, another more convincing interpretation carries the day and becomes the orthodox interpretation for colleagues in the field. Much of what we learn as history consists of the current assertions of strong and competent individuals about a particular segment of the past.

A historian's assertion may be widely accepted over a long period of time, but eventually it becomes just another historical source, and a secondary source at that most of the time. During its popular period the assertion rallies adherents and followers much as religions do. Followers may develop long and sophisticated works defending the assertion of historical faith to which they have subscribed. They may be convinced of the superior merits of the assertion over all other historical frameworks, but almost inevitably a more viable framework emerges. Human reason and logic can build an airtight case for each passing historical assertion. Human reason and logic, to be sure, play a large part in the conception and description of a historical frame, but they are not the ultimate source of a history. Sober reason and logic are too humiliated by the historical imponderables.

It seems to me that the ultimate source of history is the will of the historian to assert his particular faith in humanity and the will of people to accept the assertion. To be sure, he must have sources; he must employ considerable time and thought in order to understand and evaluate them; he must tax his reason to produce a convincing framework to present his views; in the end he sets down statements based upon his own convictions about man and his world. In the end he wills to be human, to present his own conception of humanity. If his conception convinces many, he is honored as a historian.

CHAPTER 2

THE BIBLE AND HISTORY

THE Christian Bible is a sourcebook of history, not a history book. Although it provides the chief and sometimes the only sources for the history of Palestine in the biblical period, it was not written as a history and is, at best, a compilation of sources. When historians use biblical material, they are faced with all the imponderables of ancient historical sources plus the added difficulties of traditional development, textual variation, and theological orientation.

THE IMPONDERABLES OF THE BIBLICAL SOURCES

Recording

Unfortunately for historians and for us, the biblical sources were not simply written down. Most of them passed through centuries of written transmission and re-editing, and before that some of them had passed through even longer periods of oral transmission. The classical example is the book of Genesis, which is by critical tradition divided among three sources called J, E, and P. Some scholars think they can see even more sources and talk about J_1, J_2, and the like. It is generally agreed by biblical scholars that the earliest editor or redactor worked at least some four hundred years before the last, and some of the events described are commonly assigned to a period at least eight hundred years before the time of the first editor.

The historian has before him the end-product of centuries of oral and written transmission. While some traces of transmission are detectable, the identification of the steps of transmission back to the original event are irrecoverable. There is no agreement, even, on how large a role has been played by oral transmission. If we ask what were the original events which gave rise to the Genesis traditions, many scholars tell us that the events behind the first eleven chapters of Genesis are unhistorical or quite unrecoverable,[1] while the rest of Genesis is legendary. That means that there was a nucleus of historical action which gave rise to the story, but this cannot be satisfactorily defined.

If the original events cannot be recovered, what about the contributions of the editors? If we do not know the stages through which the oral tradition developed over eight centuries, it is hard to decide what contributions the first editor made. Did he merely transcribe oral tradition, or did he add something substantial to the tradition? Why did the latest editor not entirely re-edit the work? Some of these questions are fiercely debated by biblical scholars. Do the sources of Genesis have any historical significance if even the character of the events themselves cannot be clearly perceived? The controversy between scholars who answer this question affirmatively and those whose answer is negative is discussed in the fourth chapter. For the historian such debates bring to focus the imponderables which unfold as he takes a closer look at the recording and transmission of the biblical sources.

Description

If a description of the events which gave rise to the Genesis traditions cannot be satisfactorily recovered, any evaluation of such description is obviously precluded. This does not mean that the extant traditional descriptions may not be evaluated. The historian can assess, for example, the extent to which traditions about the biblical patriarchs are overlaid with anachronisms, but here we are concerned with the value of descriptions which provide a reasonably concise historical context. Not all biblical sources are as historically inscrutable as Genesis. At times, sources approach the level of a first-rate eyewitness account. The classical example is the court history of David (2 Samuel 9–20), but even this description provides only one perspective on selected events.

If we turn to the works of the Deuteronomist and the Chronicler, for example, we are still dealing with descriptions of events written down in final form for the most part centuries after the event. Here historians are more positive about the possibilities of learning something of the events described, but also these sources bristle with problems. The description is often of such a nature that there is no way to settle the divisions of scholarly opinion about its significance. One scholar is convinced that a description is completely aetiological. That is, it is a tale invented to explain the presence of a prominent element in the story such as the name of a city, the location of a tree, or the origin of a traditional practice. For example, some believe that the story of Lot's wife turning to a pillar of salt was a tale invented to explain a prominent salt pillar near the south end of the Dead Sea; others see the event as representing an incident in a great catastrophe which convulsed the southern end of the Dead Sea. Again, one scholar is awed by the perspicacity of a prophet who foresees an impending event. Another is convinced that the prophetic details were added by an editor after the event.

At times the same or similar events are described in two sources. Frequently details vary and sometimes the descriptions are rather contradictory. In the case of one description of the conquest under Joshua, for example, the conquest is seen as a rapid, successful thrust; another source describes it as much slower and more gradual. Some scholars consider the former description more authentic, others the latter. Details of this debate are discussed in Chapter 4. In nearly every description scholars debate to what extent the editor has spiritualized, expurgated, or otherwise altered the circumstances of the original event. Such are the imponderables associated with descriptions of events in biblical sources.

Language

Did you ever read a passage in the Bible and say to yourself, "Why, that doesn't make any sense!" and reread it only to come to the same conclusion? Such an experience need not always be attributed to your ignorance. At times the biblical language is not understood, or the particular text may be preserved for us in a corrupt or distorted form. It may seem strange to find the King James Version of Job's cry, "yet in my flesh shall I see God," changed in the Revised Standard Version to, "then without my flesh shall I see God." The explanation in the RSV footnote is honest: the meaning of this verse is uncertain. Before we face the problem of understanding the words we must attempt to discover the uncorrupted original text.

The determination of the original text is not always easy. The fact that the Bible is the most copied, translated, and reproduced book in the world is not an unmixed blessing. To sort out the thousands of manuscripts of the texts and versions, to establish text types, families, and recensions, and to isolate what appears to be the text most faithful to the original becomes more insuperable as new material regularly streams in. It is a task, in fact, which is being turned over to computers as far as this is possible.

Occasionally in the Dead Sea Scrolls there are texts which may have been written within a century of the autograph, or original document, but usually we have copies of the texts which are centuries later than the final re-edition of the text, and often there are divergences between one manuscript and another. The words of which manuscript are closer to the original or the final redaction? At times there are further complications. Before the Dead Sea Scrolls were discovered, the earliest Hebrew texts of the Old Testament belonged to the ninth and tenth centuries A.D. There were Greek translations of the Old Testament in manuscripts of the fourth and fifth centuries A.D. Where they diverged, which should be used: the Hebrew text or its Greek translation with manuscripts antedating those of the Hebrew by some five hundred years? Since the discovery of the Dead Sea Scrolls, we have learned that the answer is not so simple—indeed, that we were not even asking the right question. We have learned that before the standardization of the texts which were available to us before the Scrolls, there were traditions (recensions) of the Old Testament text carried forward in Babylonia, Palestine, and Egypt, each of which had its own peculiarities. Now scholars are discussing how to determine the original text from among these traditions, or recensions.[2]

When we have come as close to the final edition of the text as we can, we have the imponderables of biblical language. We mentioned in the preceding chapter that one prominent biblical scholar estimates that only about half the book of Job can be translated with assurance. We are in a better position with other portions of the Bible, but every year there are new meanings to words being brought to light through persistent scholarly research or through light from newly discovered or published texts. When we can offer a translation, there are still the problems of the lack of exact correspondence between ancient and modern words, which we also mentioned in the previous chapter, and it is exceedingly difficult for us to let the ancient words paint a picture of the ancient world rather than the world which words ordinarily call to our consciousness. These are some of the problems of understanding related to biblical language, impressive imponderables that a large core of biblical scholars spend lifetimes attempting to fathom.

Audience

It is extremely difficult to determine the audience for which the biblical sources were written. Each of the countless oral and written re-editions involves reinterpretation for a new, contemporary audience. This is the same process which is continued every time a modern scholar sets down a new interpretation of the biblical traditions for his own day. In certain instances it is possible, at least in part, to distinguish features of a particular redaction for a particular occasion, such as the Deuteronomic reforms of King Josiah's reign, but in most instances scholars are far from agreement even upon the date of the final redaction of a given source. Some of the books of the prophets, for example, are attributed to the seventh century B.C. by some scholars, to the fourth and third by others.

Sometimes we can see something of the character of the audience from the concerns of the redactor, even if we can only vaguely specify the audience chronologically. In general, the audience remains at least as vague and impersonal as the editor. To be sure, the sources contain dramatic portrayals of many individuals, but even in these instances it must be asked whether their characters have been polished for a particular audience or tarnished for another. To penetrate to the individual human characters of the biblical sources, of the editors, of the audiences is an immense and largely imponderable task.

Theological Perspective

A final imponderable, the great imponderable of the Bible, is its theological perspective. The Bible does not consist of a historian's assertion built upon his evaluation of the sources, but the biblical sources do make a clear, nearly unified, and unmistakable assertion. This assertion is cast and recast in the long process through which the biblical traditions developed, but at bottom it remains unchanged. It is the assertion of the conviction that in all events described God is working out the salvation of his people.

The God who created the world called upon Abraham to father his chosen people. They migrated westward from Mesopotamia but had to serve as slaves of the Egyptians for centuries before they were permitted by God to settle in Palestine, the land he had promised them. After a process of consolidation, they were able to take over the rule of the land. Rulers and people often forgot God. God punished them and, when they repented, restored them. Their wickedness became so persistent that God permitted the nations to destroy them and lead his people into captivity. He preserved a remnant from captivity, which he returned to Palestine. They restored the temple and worship of God. Finally, God sent a Savior to this people to rescue and redeem them, to claim them as his people once and for all. This Savior was God's own son, whose mission was to redeem his people and the entire world.

REACTIONS TO THE BIBLICAL IMPONDERABLES

What assertions is it possible for contemporary historians of the biblical period to make in the face of these imponderables? Here we may characterize superficially four representative reactions of contemporary historians to the imponderables of the biblical sources. It goes without saying that any assertions are inevitably going to be partial and unsatisfactory in the face of such vast imponderables. It is also to be noted that each of these reactions is an assertion, an assertion of belief or faith, that a particular evaluation of the sources and a particular framework expresses an understanding of value to the historian's contemporaries.[3]

The Strict Secularist

The first is the assertion of the strict secularist. Secularization seems to be a major trend with its results penetrating nearly all elements of modern life. This has been welcomed by certain quarters of the Christian Church with the contention that the substance of the Christian proclamation has continuing relevance for secularized man. Against the view that something of the substance of the Christian faith has validity in a secular context stands the "strict" secularist. Analysis of the historical sources and conclusions vary radically as the viability of the Church's proclamation for secularized man is affirmed or denied. The difference may be seen by comparing the views of the strict secularist in this section with those of the demythologizer in the next. Note that both begin with an assertion or creed. Very roughly, it is either affirmed or denied that God has a counterpart in the secular age. Either what traditional theological language talked about had some substance which can still be talked about in secular terms or it never had any substance, was vacuity, and all talk about it was self-deceptive.

The strict secularist begins with the categorical denial that anything suprahistorical is involved in biblical history or any other history. As he looks at contemporary history, he sees nothing in the sources that would suggest a suprahuman dimension to the events described: no God, no divine force, no predetermined destiny, no devil, no malevolent force, no predetermined catastrophe. There is no reason to think that the past was in any way different from the present. Certainly we understand man and his environs better today than ever before. In fact, there are still pockets of people who preserve the past for us to examine today. These primitives help us to understand the superstitions, fetishes, and traditional behavior of the past. Even in rather sophisticated circles of the present day there is much of the cult of magic and superstition, of religious faith and creedalism, which reflects the same kinds of human deception described in the Bible.

If we examine the ancient world, we find in the Near East that sources for history very similar to those of the Bible are available for the ancient Egyptians and Mesopotamians, and related material is found in the early literature of Europe and the Middle and Far East. The value in the study of biblical sources, like other ancient sources, is to shed light on the vestigial elements of superstition in our present world. A likely framework to be employed by such a historian is one which outlines the successive stages of man's evolutionary development. As man grows in skills and self-understanding through the centuries, he gradually throws off the shackles of religious superstition; his need to create a god to worship declines. Instead, he has as a foundation the growing scientific understanding of the world and man.

This position is criticized by other historians. It is in the first place subhistorical. It does not take the ancient world seriously on its own terms. There is no serious attempt to discover what the sources meant when they were written. To denigrate what was going on in the ancient thought world as superstition is not to have understood the men of antiquity. They were no less human than present-day followers of Zodiac signs or believers in something suprahistorical.

Further, this position is often coupled with a rigid and unrealistic view of the evolution of man. The evolutionary structure when applied to the short chronology of historical time is virtually meaningless. Several thousand years ago there was a spectrum from primitivism to sophistication not unlike what existed at the beginning of the present century. Some of today's less developed nations had a glorious and highly developed past.

This view also tends to underestimate the differences between man and the material world. The methods of the natural and social sciences are not the same, and both differ from those of the humanities. Strict secularism was nurtured in the era when the natural sciences were a new, exciting phenomenon, when science was expected to provide a new way of life. Today we have a more sober appreciation of its limitations: there are human dimensions that cannot be dealt with successfully in the laboratory and the test tube. It is significant to note that the strict secularist view is espoused today especially among students of primitive and comparative religion. These disciplines arose as part of the positivistic developments of the last century and appear as a rather anachronistic perpetuation of such methodology.

Finally, the assertion that there is no suprahistorical dimension is simply not accepted by many of the secularist's contemporaries. The presence of the historical imponderables described above implies that there is something about man that escapes his powers of observation, his understanding. This is tantamount to saying that there is an extrahuman, possibly suprahuman, dimension. Beyond this, the very assertion of the secularist historian is a statement of belief or faith—faith that he can go beyond his sources to a framework which presents viable understandings of man. To state that there is no suprahistorical dimension is to make a suprahistorical statement, for such a statement cannot be clearly demonstrated from within history and its sources: there are too many imponderables. Only a believer can make historical assertions; it takes faith to write history.

The Demythologizer

The demythologizer attempts to be at the same time a secularist historian and a believer. Rudolf Bultmann, doyen of the demythologizers, has devoted a lifetime of effort to secularizing the biblical sources. His program has involved a stripping away of the mythological world of the New Testament so that its message can be understood by modern man. This effort has led him to conclude that the purpose of the New Testament authors was to call man to a radical faith. This call Bultmann has attempted to present in the secular language of existential philosophy. Radical faith becomes an authentic self-understanding.

There is only one element in the New Testament which Bultmann failed to demythologize radically, the cross of Christ, and that element he considered crucial for faith. Radical faith therefore depends on a historical act of God linked with Jesus of Nazareth. If we ask how much more we can learn about Jesus from the sources, Bultmann is quite skeptical: the sources reveal nothing finally dependable about Jesus beyond the fact that he is the Revealer.[4]

Bultmann's students and critics have had trouble putting together his program of secularization and his assertion that the self-understanding of faith depends upon Jesus of Nazareth. If self-understanding is at bottom "the shattering and negating of all human self-assertion and all human norms and evaluations,"[5] why is such faith necessarily linked to Jesus? Is not such self-understanding possible for man as man, for secular man apart from Jesus? Bultmann replies that such self-understanding is possible in principle for secular man, but that possibility is negated by the fall. Secular man can only achieve despair, from which he can be released only by an act of God.

Most of Bultmann's colleagues and students have not been satisfied by this answer. There is no basic quarrel with Bultmann's conception of faith. The definition by Karl Barth is closely followed by Bultmann, Tillich, and their students. There is also general agreement that such faith is compromised if it is in any way dependent on the results of historical research. The problem is the linking of this faith with Jesus of Nazareth. If a link with Jesus is essential, how is Bultmann able to claim that faith is independent of historical research or that his program of historical research has been successful in secularizing (demythologizing) the New Testament, freeing it from suprahistorical presuppositions? To say that fallen man does not have the possibility of self-understanding denies the autonomy of historical research and of faith.

An obvious reaction is to deny that there is any necessary link between faith and Jesus of Nazareth. The shortest step in this direction was taken by Paul Tillich, who affirms that "absolute faith" is possible for men who have never heard of Jesus; at the same time he is convinced that such faith found perfect expression in Jesus, "that the New Testament picture of Jesus as the Christ has saving power for those who are grasped by it, no matter how much or how little can be traced to the historical figure who is called Jesus of Nazareth."[6]

Others, like Schubert Ogden,[7] are more radical in their rejection of the link between faith and Jesus. The cross of Christ is just another element of mythology in need of secularization. The insistence on Jesus as essential to faith vitiates the possibility of faith for every man and makes a mockery of the universal grace of God. Existentialist philosophy affirms self-understanding as a gift in essentially the same way that this may be learned through the picture of Jesus in the New Testament. To say that faith has an essential link with Jesus leads to a radical distortion of faith or a denial of the autonomy of historical research vis-à-vis Jesus or both.

Still more radical are the so-called Christian atheists or God-is-dead theologians. While rejecting the link between faith and Jesus, Ogden affirms God as a nonobjective reality which man experiences.[8] The Christian atheists insist that all talk about and experience of God is impossible. The New Testament Jesus has "disappeared from our history."[9] This is merely a manifestation of the basic reality of the death of God in our times. Faith which "nostalgically seeks an historical past" must be rejected.[10] True Christian faith is a present, human act.[11] "To the extent that we imagine Jesus in his traditional Christian form we are closed to his contemporary presence."[12] The experience of the contemporary presence is as yet unfulfilled. Meanwhile, the Christian atheists wait out in the world and "talk about becoming Jesus in and to the world."[13] They are convinced that if Christian faith appears, it will appear within the arena of history, in the lives of men like themselves.[14] If faith is to be rediscovered, it will be within the ordinary lives of men—the end-product of secularization.

While some of Bultmann's successors were moving to the "left," denying the necessary link of faith with Jesus, others were moving to the "right." For them the Christian faith is dependent not merely on the early Church's affirmation of Jesus Christ but upon the continuity of that affirmation with the life and teachings of Jesus of Nazareth. If historical research should cast strong doubts upon this continuity, the Christian faith would be rendered baseless. The concern to divorce faith from the shifting postulational results of historical research involves, to use the words of James M. Robinson, an "unbelieving flight to security, i.e., the reverse of faith."[15]

While agreeing with Barth, Bultmann, and Tillich that historical research cannot confirm the Christian faith, those of the right do give a much more prominent role to historical research. Against Bultmann and others they maintain that historical research could disconfirm the Christian faith if serious doubts were cast upon the continuity between Jesus and the affirmation of the early Church. New Testament research cannot present evidence to prove the validity of the Christian faith, but it is not impossible that it might turn up evidence tending to disprove it. To deny this is to deny the elements of risk and paradox that are essential to faith.

The greater prominence given to historical research may be seen in the treatment of the life of Jesus. Barth, Bultmann, and Tillich were extremely skeptical about what could be said about the life and teachings of Jesus himself. The evidence does not permit a sound judgment upon the continuity between Jesus and the affirmations of the early Church in the New Testament. This skepticism was a reaction against the Jesus research of the last century in which Jesus came out with too much of a nineteenth-century character and teachings closely akin to those of his modern biographers.

In the last decade there has been a resurgence of research on the life and teachings of Jesus. A monument in this resurgence has been James M. Robinson's *A New Quest of the Historical Jesus*, conveniently suggesting the tab "new questers" for those on the "right."[16] The new quest repudiates the methodology of the earlier quest; what was left after a positivistic elimination of supernatural elements from the sources was not the historical Jesus but a mutilation of the early Church's picture of Jesus.[17] The skepticism of the dialectic theologians was justified vis-à-vis the earlier quest. The new quest is based on a new methodology, a different approach to historical research, a new hermeneutic.[18] This new method of interpretation has developed in close relation to recent trends in philosophical thought, particularly existentialism. The views of such men as Martin Heidegger, Karl Jaspers, and R. G. Collingwood have been particularly influential.

In the new quest, history "does not consist in external facts but in the purposes and meanings of selves," and a self is "constituted by commitment to a context."[19] The detachment and objectivity of the nineteenth-century historian is replaced by engagement. The historian understands the past when his own self-understanding comes under its influence. This new approach to historical sources is what makes possible a new quest for the historical Jesus. If the picture of Jesus in the New Testament sources was not amenable to recovery of facts about the life of Jesus, the affirmation of the early Church in the New Testament is precisely concerned with the selfhood of Jesus. The

New Testament sources preserve just that kind of material which is of interest to the new questers. The new historians as historians confront men with the selfhood of Jesus. The presentation of Jesus, the product of their research, like the preachment of the early Church and of the Christian Church today, is a call to faith, authentic self-understanding. If the self-understanding of Jesus in the New Testament agrees with the self-understanding discovered by the new research, then skepticism about the historical Jesus can be dismissed.

There is a vigorous internal dialogue between and among the various camps that have developed among the demythologizers. More general criticism is often cast as a heresy trial, but there do seem to be a number of places at which a historian finds the demythologizers vulnerable. Of course, each criticism applies with different force to the various camps.

The basic method of demythologizing may be considered subhistorical. To be sure, the biblical sources must be critically examined to determine as far as possible what events were involved and how traditions about them developed. The demythologizers go one step further and ask, "What would a twentieth-century observer see if he were watching the ancient event? What meaning would it have for him?" Such "playing first-century A.D.," as Krister Stendahl calls it,[20] is neither realistic nor historical. It de-emphasizes concern for what biblical people thought and said and understood within the mythical world in which they lived. Who cares what *I* would have thought witnessing a first-century A.D. event! It is understandings of these people and events on their own terms, within their own world, which provides the basis for a contemporary comprehension of biblical times. In contrast, the process of demythologizing leads to the discovery of "the empty shell of a once vital faith."[21]

Another way to state this criticism is to call the results of demythologizing subpersonal. The impression frequently left by demythologizers is that their assertions are mere repetitions of the biblical assertions about what God is doing in biblical history. The people and events themselves are divested of humanity by stripping away the actual mythological world in which they lived. We can know virtually nothing about Jesus beyond the fact that he lived in Palestine in the first century A.D., though we can know more about his message as preached in the early Church. Rather than strip away from Jesus all that belongs to the mythical thought world of his day, is it not more faithful to history to honor the descriptions of his words and acts as observed by his contemporaries and attempt to see in these something of the character of the man himself? Is it people and events which are the bearers of history, or is it meanings behind events and people?

This question is crucial. If our main purpose is searching out meanings behind events, we are not far from seeking out universal truths, the task of a philosopher, not a historian. If we follow the new questers in their search for the purposes and meanings of selves in their contextual commitment and "grasp the possibilities of existence which have come to expression in the past and which are repeatable in the present and future,"[22] have we done more than apprehended a universal truth? If we have used the methods of the demythologizer, with their subhistorical and subpersonal results, the answer is clearly negative. This seems to be the crux of the problem for the demythologizers. In the present they are existentially concerned about self-understanding (their definition of faith), selfhood, and commitment to a context. In dealing with historical material, their methods lead to the elimination of the ancient context and the destruction of ancient selves.

If study of the ancient sources is to be a historical rather than a philosophical task, it might be expected that methodology should aim, not at elimination of the myth of the ancient world, but at its increased comprehension, for only thus can the ancient selves and contexts be elucidated. Unless the ancient material is merely a springboard or inspiration for a universal truth, it is hard to see how apprehension of ancient selves is possible without the arduous task of attempting to understand those selves in their own contexts. This involves a detailed comprehension of precisely those elements that demythologizing proposes to eliminate.

This points up the problems of the new quest. How do the new questers propose to understand the self and context of Jesus? If not simply through the eyes of the early Church, how do the new questers hope to make advances over the old? In historical research, judgments about self-understanding and contexts come as a result of painstaking, detailed research, precisely the objective, factual kind of research which led the earlier questers to such skeptical results. Conclusions about motivation, purpose, self-understanding, and context are always among the least verifiable historical conclusions. How do the new questers propose to reach assured conclusions about Jesus' self-understanding? The fact is that their conclusions can hardly command greater assent than their predecessors; the new questers' conclusions about Jesus' self-understanding are as close to their own theological views as the earlier questers' conclusions were to theirs.

Perhaps something of an understanding of Christian atheists is possible in this context. William Hamilton juxtaposes talk about waiting and the death of God with following—indeed, becoming—Jesus in the world.[23] Is there behind this the conviction that the early Church's apprehension is meaningless today? The historians have been unable to get at Jesus by the old quest or the new; but something is clear from the sources: Jesus out in his world. Part of the waiting may be for a way to affirm Jesus in our secularized world. The demythologizing program has shown that this cannot be accomplished by attempting to construct a secular first-century A.D. Jesus.

These criticisms are possible from within the demythologizers' own framework. It is also possible to criticize the framework itself, and this seems required by what has been said above about the imponderables of history and the faith of the historian. The purpose of the demythologizing program has been to distill from historical sources what can contribute to one's self-understanding. Self-understanding is considered in an existential context often with Freudian or Jungian connotations. From the side of history, it is subject to debate whether such self-understanding is the primary goal of any kind of historical source analysis—unless history and biography are confused. A study of history is more likely to expand than to clarify one's own little world, and there are no guarantees that self-understanding will be enhanced in the larger world. One's world is more likely to be complicated, and one's role more difficult to assess and affirm.

From the side of faith, the definition of faith as self-understanding, something secure from the vagaries of historical research, has been the overriding assumption of the dialectical theologians for decades. Only the new questers are willing to subject faith to the risk of historical research—to the extent that the early Church's picture of Jesus could be disconfirmed by such research. If faith is defined as self-understanding in modern subjectivist terms, are not the Christian atheists right in their contention that there is no more need for a divine need-filler?[24] The problems of self-understanding can be entrusted to psychologists, sociologists, psychiatrists, and the like. Indeed, this definition of faith is at least partly behind the importation of so many of these specialists into seminaries these days. Whatever their success in dealing with problems of individuals, it is hardly with such self-understanding that history or historic Christianity has been or should be primarily concerned.

History has to do with broader contexts. History will not make much over the current crop of psychiatrists and the lives they have redirected, or re-misdirected. Even the private lives of the current bearers of history will not bulk large in the history books of the twentieth century, except perhaps in a psychiatrist's history. Faith does not exist apart from history. The security of the natural repetitions of natural cycles does not require what has historically been considered faith. If faith does not exist apart from history, it too has to do with broader contexts than self-understanding. Faith attaches people to historical groups, to their affirmations and aspirations. These span great distances of time and space. Such attachments can deal with problems of self-understanding perhaps more effectively than the adjustments within the individual's little world proposed by the psychiatrist.

Faith in the context of history has elements of risk, of daring, of affirming something bigger than one's own little world. Faith faces the imponderables of history, and all their implications for the puniness of the human intellect, and affirms an understanding—but not a final one. Understandings will change and develop, but the affirmation is the best the historian can make at the moment. Such affirmations are made in the face of human limitations in dealing with historical sources and specifically the historian's imperfect grasp of his own role and control of his own idiosyncrasies in particular historical affirmations. Far from being defined as self-understanding, faith in a historical context specifically affirms substantial limitations—or, if you will, failures—of self-understanding. A part of the historian's faith is his stamina, his courage to affirm despite limitations of self-understanding.

If an element of affirmation beyond self-understanding is accepted, then the element of myth or poetry cannot be entirely excluded. The things beyond our grasp we can express only poetically or mythically. If the kinds of pictures used by ancient poets do not speak to us, perhaps in place of demythologizing should come attempts to present these elements in new poems and pictures. This is precisely what many of the Christian atheists are doing in their preoccupation with literature and drama.

Another important trend among the demythologizers is preoccupation with language, which is not under consideration here. Its basic assumption is Heidegger's view that language is the house (prison?) of being.[25] If what has been said about poetic attempts to affirm what is beyond our grasp is accepted, such an assumption must be emphatically denied. The view of Mircea Eliade seems much more realistic: certain things exist even if words for them are lacking.[26]

While affirming a lot of truth in what the Christian atheists have to say, it is tempting to say that for them everything is dead except the little world they affirm. Some even imprison themselves within the vocabulary they know how to use. As they see it, the world of history is dead for most Americans—whether it be Greece and Rome or first-century A.D. Palestine. If Americans are to be helped, this help must come from within the little world they affirm. Is it excluded to consider help in the direction of an exciting, expanding world—in time and space, in history? Here it is fitting to note that the demythologizers have had a rather limited historical preoccupation with the historical Jesus and his affirmation by the early Church. Their concerns with history have been shaped by this particular historical problem as they have defined it. The definition of the problem could itself be better rounded from the broader perspective of the sweep of Near Eastern and biblical history together with that of two millennia of church history. With this observation it is fitting to turn to the reactions of a third group to the imponderables of the biblical sources.

The Biblical Theologian

As the term suggests, the biblical theologian is one who attempts to affirm the theological perspective of the Bible itself. God is acting to save his people throughout biblical history. This culminates in the sending of his son to redeem the world. Stress is placed on God's great acts. If we turn back to the events at Southampton, among all the things that happened on the beach those three days, only a few connected events were considered a Happening. Perhaps a number of people on the beach were celebrating some of the great events of their lives—a honeymoon, relaxing while writing a profound book, striking up a romance, escaping from the eyes of the law after a notable escapade. Yet all of these events were nonhappenings. Only one Happening was taking place at Southampton beach. So the biblical theologian looks at his biblical sources. In this repository are great Happenings in which God revealed his way and plan of salvation for his people. His people preserve in their traditional memory these great acts. They become a credo, a creed which they repeat on great national occasions. We believe that God delivered us from Egypt, gave us the promised land, and so on. Beside these, all other events pale into insignificance.

This group has been concerned with the critical evaluation of the biblical sources. What were the events and happenings which God's people affirmed in their *credo*? This *credo* was frequently part of a covenant ceremony between God and his people, and much attention has been devoted to the elements, forms, and sources of the biblical covenants in which God promises to be Israel's God, and Israel to be his faithful people.[27] This group has tended to be much less skeptical about the extent to which the events and persons of the Bible can be recovered from the sources—recovered in the context of their own times, not as demythologized moderns. To that end this group has also tended much more to stress the importance of a knowledge of the comparative history and archaeology of the ancient Near East. Such knowledge is of value in providing a perspective of the theater in which God undertook his great acts.

Once the broad perspective has been achieved, God's great acts can be communicated directly to modern man. We are confronted "with the person of the living God and of his Son" and "with the activity of men in whom we see ourselves, so that the distance between the biblical generations and our generation is bridged and we become participants in the original history in order to participate rightly in our own."[28] History then and now is "the interacting 'challenge-and-response' movement between God and man which God is directing to his own good."[29] Faith is the affirmation of this encounter today as it was in the times of the Bible. "Theology and history are inseparable, and both require an act of self-transcendence . . . to comprehend both Event and the Word which expounds it."[30]

The crucial problem for a historian facing the perspective of the biblical theologian is similar to the one he confronted with the demythologizer: How shall I deal with the assertion that there is a necessary link between God's great acts and my participating "rightly" in my own history? How shall I deal with the assertion of a necessary link between Jesus and self-understanding? The biblical theologian's method of dealing with historical sources is the one which might have been expected of the demythologizer, for it attempts to get at the understandings of ancient people within their own worlds insofar as this is possible through literary and archaeological sources. The biblical theologian has affirmed the first task of the secular historian.

At this point, however, the secular historian and the biblical theologian part company. The biblical theologian wants modern man to see himself in the men of the biblical period as they encounter God. By participating in biblical history we learn "rightly" to participate in our own. The biblical theologian does not ask: What would a twentieth-century A.D. observer have noted in first-century A.D. Palestine? He asks: What would I have experienced had I been a follower of Moses or Joshua or Jesus? When we have learned to act in a first-century A.D. drama, we will know how to act today.

When a practical implementation of the biblical theologian's program is contemplated, there seem to be some internal inconsistencies. Consider the problem of most Christian laymen attempting to play first-century A.D. Even mature and sophisticated historians could spend lifetimes disagreeing about important elements in the drama. Even if they could agree, the result would be the best hypothesis on the evidence available. Is re-enacting such a problematic role likely to help us "rightly" to participate in our own history? What I suspect has happened in many instances where biblical theology has been affirmed is that the acts of God affirmed have been largely stripped of their biblical and historical context. That God interacted with his people has become almost another eternal truth, for it is difficult to see, for example, how the description of the details of God's action for Israel at the Red Sea has any counterparts in my life or in the historical world I affirm. The biblical theologian's assertion that God can be known only in concrete historical situations, not from the abstract world of ideas, must often be reversed in application to the present. Since I cannot see precisely the hand of God in current historical situations, I can only affirm abstractly that he is acting.

But is he? Another internal problem is precisely this: the emphasis on the great acts of God leaves a great many historical events and vast eras of historical time in a twilight of "never-never land." In fact, part of the biblical perspective, biblical theology, if you will, is that Jesus' contemporaries were convinced that God had not spoken for centuries. The concern of the biblical theologians for a current awareness of God's activity in history is partly undercut by emphasis on a few great acts of God. In fact, it is not foreign to the biblical perspective to say that we are living in an interlude between God's last great act of salvation in the first-century A.D. and the time he returns to bring this salvation to fruition. The last two thousand years are the last moment before the rule of God becomes manifest.

Turning to criticism from the outside, the very assertion that one can participate in the original biblical history is deceptively oversimplified. It has been noted that the biblical sources contain complicated traditions about historical events which developed over centuries. The end-product is far from unadulterated history. Rather than with "the original history," we are confronted with a mixture of cosmology, myth, apocalyptic, and history often in covenantal form mediated through a ritual context.[31] The great biblical acts of God have historical elements but are far from historical events as we moderns understand them.

The most devastating attack on biblical theologians can be mounted by the Christian atheists, but similar attacks can be made by other demythologizer camps or even by the strict secularists. If there is much truth to the view that traditional language about God is dead, that there is the experience of the absence of God,[32] then the program of the biblical theologians is in serious difficulty. Precisely the great acts of God are the biblical elements which are farthest from having any contemporary counterpart. The two positions are diametrically opposed: it is/is not possible for us to empathize with biblical experiences of the action of God; it is/is not possible for us to be confronted in our own lives with the activity of the living God. It seems doubtful that the Old Testament credo speaks more to modern man than the creed of the early Church. While the truth probably lies somewhere between the extremities of these positions, time is probably on the side of the Christian atheists: as secularization progresses fewer and fewer will feel it possible to perceive God acting in their history after having relived the great acts of God.

From the historian's perspective all these criticisms at bottom say that the approach of the biblical theologian is subhistorical. The study of the biblical and historical sources has not led to the proposal of a framework by which understandings of biblical events can be communicated to modern men. The approach itself seems to demand a framework which fails to take most history and most human achievements seriously. Most human action pales into insignificance because it is not involved in one of God's great acts or related to God's chosen people. Even in these great events man often appears as a tool in God's hand, and God is said to have done great things through his chosen instruments. Such a perspective might be acceptable to some theologians, but the historian has a broader and deeper interest in men and human events. His assertions about these human events comprise history. If there is a divine dimension of the past which can be communicated to modern man, would it not more likely be found in the more ordinary events of the past, events for which he finds counterparts in his own situation? The biblical theologian affirms that God reveals himself in history; if this statement has any contemporary truth, the biblical theologian should be able to produce a convincing history of the biblical period for our times. Reproduction of the biblical perspective is only the first step of the way toward production of a history of biblical times.

The Dogmatist

The final assertion about the biblical imponderables to be considered is that of what may be called the biblical dogmatist. This approach, which dominated biblical studies less than a century ago, is now largely eclipsed, but perhaps it has enough supporters today to justify a brief description. The dogmatist looks upon the Bible first of all as an inspired work. It is a book written by men specially moved by God to set down the truths which God wanted to communicate to men, to convey his plan of salvation for man. Some dogmatists limit divine inspiration (that is, material free from human error) to God's plan of salvation while others claim that the entire Bible is free from any kind of error. These latter consider any kind of literary or historical criticism of the biblical sources out of the question, as subjecting God's truth to imperfect human judgment and criticism.

This means that there is no place for a historian in the modern sense. Instead, there is need for a dogmatician, for the Bible is viewed by this group as a repository of truths rather than collections of historical sources. The task of the dogmatician is to isolate, list, organize, and classify the truths contained in the Bible. What does the Bible have to say about God, the Holy Spirit, angels, hell, judgment day, the Sabbath day, love, hate, peace, and so on? The history of God's saving acts is affirmed, not so much as historical events but as propositions to be accepted as true. If there are imponderables about God or man, these are unimportant, for what God wanted us to know and what is sufficient for our salvation is contained in the Bible.

In addition to being considered a repository of God's truths, the Bible is taken as a book of moral instructions. Various lessons for life may be learned from the events and stories of the Bible. These are hardly ever the lessons of history but the lessons of a pious morality. Learn from the story of Abraham and Lot that one must avoid bad company. Stick with the good people. From the story of the Prodigal Son learn to forgive wayward children. The Bible becomes a code of rules for Christian behavior and conduct.

If the earlier approaches were considered subhistorical, the dogmatist's approach should be considered nonhistorical. The dogmatician would insist that his approach is historical, for all events as described in the Bible actually happened in history as described, including such things as the miracles of Jesus. But these are stated dogmatisms not subject to historical investigation and verification. The historical process is denied. The historian's generation-by-generation rewriting of biblical history for his day is impossible for the biblical dogmatist.

These ideas about truths deserve attention. The first three approaches did not use the concept of truth, at least in the objective sense here meant. The earlier approaches would in fact deny that a historian can approach objective truth by any of their methods. An objective truth is one that stands apart from man, remains true no matter what he may say about it, remains true for all time. Historians operate within history, within the human framework. To the extent that they introduce objective truths into their source evaluations or into the frameworks of their assertions, to that extent they cease to be historians. Truths for the earlier groups consist in subjective, personal truths primarily, what is true for me. The historian is concerned about what is true in the human context, what is true for man, not apart from him. He learns that man constantly changes, always remains partly imponderable to himself and his peers.

The historian will also question the use of historical biblical materials as sources for moral lessons. This, too, is based on the assumption that unchanging truths can be derived from the Bible. It is also based on the dogmatist's thinking in whites and blacks without shades of gray. Some actions are usually right, others usually wrong, but most of them involve shades of gray.

Here we may pause to ask whether lessons are to be derived from the study of historical sources or from historians' assertions. It has been common for historians to speak of the lessons of history. In the past few centuries many historians thought that they had clearly delimited cycles through which history repeatedly passed, trends which repeated themselves again and again. It is probably impossible to get through an American university without hearing of Hegel's thesis, antithesis, and synthesis.

Today we are more hesitant to talk about historical patterns and profiting from the mistakes of history. The process of historical change is now so rapid that past patterns and circumstances seem distant and irrelevant. General Motors has been replaced by General Dynamics; General Motors has a history, but understanding General Dynamics demands an understanding of current conditions and trends. In fact, the study of history itself seems less essential today.

Vietnam may well illustrate the point. To say that America

should have learned from the French experience to avoid involvement in Vietnam is an example of the broad kind of lesson that history must be strained to teach. Circumstances have changed in the past decade. The Americans differ from the French. Vietnam is not what is was under the French, the pressures in Southeast Asia have changed radically in the past decade, and so on. On the other hand, anything that is gleaned from the history of Vietnam and about its people contributes to the success of the present American involvement in Vietnam. What are the beliefs and superstitions, the hopes and aspirations, the disappointments and fears, the manners and customs, the social stratification and economic status of the Vietnamese? The more he learns about these things, the more effective an American he will be, whatever his role in Vietnam. History, then, can tell us about particular groups of people, but dogmatic assertions about truths and morals in history are unhistorical.

We have examined some of the imponderables of the biblical sources. We have sketched four contemporary approaches to the biblical material. We have noted that each of these seems to have important inadequacies from the historian's perspective. You are perhaps at this point awaiting a description of an acceptable historical approach to the biblical material. I am afraid that I cannot point out an acceptable example, nor can I detail here what I would consider a salutary approach. Such requires no small part of a lifetime's work. I am convinced that it involves the long and difficult process of attempting to understand what biblical sources meant in their own context, on their own terms, and that this can be most effectively accomplished by the secular historian. The second step depends upon the audience for which the historian writes, be it his secular colleagues, the interested layman, or partisans in institutional religion. To the same extent that the historian analyzes and understands the pertinent segment of history, he must analyze and understand his audience.

Only then can he affirm an interpretation of the past which contributes to the current conversation, to the growth of humanity and civilization.

The origin and earliest growth of historical affirmation unfolds on the pages of the Bible. Even for a secular historian it is a source of special interest. The Christian theologian's interest continues beyond this point. He has particular interest in the series of affirmations that unfold in biblical history—as described by the secular historian. From his area of competence in the history of Christian thought and its present stance, it is his task to examine the values of those affirmations for contemporary Christianity.

This task of the theologian must be carefully distinguished from that of the biblical historian. It is my conviction that the distinction is not that the historian tells us "what it meant," and the theologian tells us "what it means." The distinction I prefer may perhaps be clarified by illustration. A few years ago a young American received his first foreign assignment from the Department of State to the capital of an Arab country. He had received the best training for such an assignment America could offer, and he had a brilliant and open mind. As he assessed his experience, he confided that there had been two major influences on his life during the course of his first assignment. The first was the ambassador under whom he served and for whom he had the highest admiration; this was reflected in the remarkable way in which his style approached that of the ambassador. The second was a profound respect for a number of Arabs, who had become close personal friends. This could be exemplified by a village head, whom he would always remember for the genuineness of his hospitality, the depth of his friendship, his singleminded integrity and fairness, and the effective power of his convictions in his dealings with his family and villagers. This power came from his commitment to affirm and implement what he understood of the divine will in his life and to accept all consequences as "from Allah." My friend felt that while he could not make the same affirmation, he was attempting to clarify an affirmation which could lead to the committed way of living he admired in the village head, a kind of affirmation he failed to find in his American context.

If we let the Arab element serve as the counterpart to the biblical-historical dimension and the ambassador and our friend as representatives of the current historical context and conversation, the historian's task is to analyze, understand, and describe the elements of the Arab context which were of such significance to the young American diplomat. To be successful the historian must understand quite clearly the young man's present context as well as a gamut of complexes from the broad world of Islam to the small world of the Arab village. He will not attempt to demythologize the Arab's convictions, state them in nontheological terms, but he will attempt to describe the world of the village head from the latter's own perspective, including what to the historian is a strange mixture of the sacred and secular. Such description may be of considerable help to the young diplomat as he attempts to clarify his own affirmation.

The role of a theologian is to consider the basic implicit and explicit affirmations (or lack of them) described by the historian—the affirmations of an Arab village head, of an American ambassador, of a young American. To what extent (if at all) and how can a young American make an affirmation comparable to the Arab he admires when he cannot accept the world of the Arab's affirmations? Can a modern man legitimately affirm something transcendental today which is a substantial counterpart of the biblical faith? Questions in this area belong to the theologian. The historian can claim no special competence in such matters.

The difficulty is that the voice of the Christian Church and the answers of theologians have been singularly unconvincing and have led to counsels of despair and skepticism—especially among the theologians themselves. This situation tempts non-theologians, including historians, to make forays into the theological sphere. The problems in this sphere concern the life and vocation of the historian at least as much as others. Indeed, if no help is forthcoming, he is obliged to decide what kinds of affirmations and attendant problems are of current importance. If he fails to do so, he becomes an antiquarian and lapses into the historicism of the last century. A viable biblical history for our generation will be written only after a viable present commitment is secured from the biblical sources.

The current Old Testament histories of Martin Noth and John Bright could be discussed in some detail.[33] They could be criticized for many major and minor defects, but at bottom they were not written with the present generation in mind.[34] In a practical way, this is almost inevitable. It takes several decades to prepare to write a biblical history; by then a new generation is on the scene. Still, I am not overpessimistic. I am confident that one or two or more will write a biblical history for the present generation. With a clear appreciation of their own limitations and of the imponderables of history, these future lights are reading works on the Bible and history with a sharp and critical eye, spending even more time reading the original sources, trying to understand the biblical world on its own terms. All evidence to the contrary, that world does come alive and speaks today.

CHAPTER 3

THE BIBLE AND ARCHAEOLOGY

WORDING titles can be a tricky business. This chapter is called "The Bible and Archaeology," not "Biblical Archaeology." The latter might have been a perfectly acceptable title if "biblical" had been clearly defined as a chronological term. Biblical archaeology is the archaeology of the biblical period as Roman archaeology is the archaeology of the Roman period. This title has been avoided because biblical archaeology has been considered in certain quarters a discipline apart, since it deals with the Bible, a book apart from all other books. For the same reason Chapter 2 was called "The Bible and History," not "Biblical History." The biblical sources bear the same kind of examination as any other historical sources, and affirmations of historians of the biblical period should not be different in kind from other historical affirmations. So biblical archaeology should stand under the same scientific and methodological disciplines as any other kind of archaeology, and its conclusions vis-à-vis its chief historical source, the Bible, should be similar in kind to conclusions about relations between other archaeological and historical material.

A rather attractive title for the previous chapter might have been "The Bible as History." A recently popular work on biblical archaeology is Werner Keller's *The Bible as History: Archaeology Confirms the Book of Books.* Any kind of link with the approach and conclusions of that book are precisely the kind of thing I wished to avoid in phrasing titles. Herr Keller tells of archaeological discoveries related to the Bible as the unfolding story of the historical accuracy of the Bible. This is clearly indicated in the English title; the German title could well be paraphrased: "The Bible Is Right after All." Further, this historical accuracy is considered a vindication of the Christian faith. The Christian faith is viable because it is based on historically accurate sources. Is this a valid conclusion? Try to keep this question in mind as we examine the character and limitations of archaeological evidence in the biblical period.

A PERSPECTIVE ON PALESTINIAN ARCHAEOLOGY

The study of ancient monuments has aroused man's curiosity from the dawn of history, but their scientific recording and excavation began only in very recent times. The first scientific excavation of an ancient site was undertaken in 1870 by Heinrich Schliemann at Hissarlik, which he identified with ancient Troy. The first excavation of a mound in Palestine was Flinders Petrie's dig at Tell el-Hesi in 1890. Actually, while excavations from that time on in Palestine were more than treasure hunts, they frequently left much to be desired from the scientific standards of their day, and some of them were strongly oriented toward biblical trove.

That Palestinian archaeology is still not much beyond infancy is demonstrated by the suddenness and rapidity with which entire new worlds of the past continue to emerge. Fifteen years ago the beginnings of urban life in the Near East were traced to the Early Bronze age in the third millennium B.C. Now an amazingly sophisticated urban world with massively fortified towns, homes with features admired even today, long trade routes, and a highly developed art is emerging in the seventh and sixth millennia B.C.—nearly twice as ancient as Early Bronze urban life.[1] Up to now there have been only the vaguest ideas about the people who occupied Palestine when the Amorites, with whom the biblical patriarchs are associated, arrived at the beginning of the second millennium B.C. That they were preceded by vast waves of invaders reaching Palestine from the steppes of Central Asia during the course of the late fourth and entire third millennia B.C. is a quite revolutionary proposal, based on evidence from the largest known cemetery in Palestine discovered in 1965.[2] The Persian period of sixth-to-fourth-century Palestine was quite enigmatic until discoveries of the last five years made it possible to date its materials with some precision and even produced a fascinating group of documents.[3] This is not the place to catalog the current flood of archaeological discoveries in Palestine, but these examples provide some indication of how rapidly our knowledge is expanding and the radical changes in perspective this entails.

Excavations in Palestine since World War II have shown that many of the conclusions of excavators before that war were radically wrong. Kathleen Kenyon has discovered that walls attributed to Joshua's time at Jericho (Pl. 1) actually belonged over a thousand years earlier[4] and that the Jebusite and Davidic defenses of Jerusalem (Pl. 2) belong nearly a millennium later than the time of David.[5] This means that with few exceptions only conclusions reached by excavators working in Palestine since 1950 who employ careful stratigraphic methods of excavation can be considered trustworthy.

The most notable exception is W. F. Albright, whose work has stood the test of time remarkably well. His standardization of the development of the pottery of Palestine from the latter part of the third millennium to the early sixth century B.C. on the basis of his excavation at Tell Beit Mirsim in southern Palestine has provided the standard chronological tool used thereafter by Palestinian archaeologists with only minor modifications.[6] In 1964 a salvage campaign was undertaken at Tell el-Fûl, just north of Jerusalem, where a new palace for Jordan's King Hussein was to be erected. Albright had excavated at the site, identified as Gibeah of Saul, in 1922 and 1933. While some colleagues were predicting that Saul's Fortress, which Albright discovered, would require redating as radical as Joshua's walls at Jericho, the results confirmed in detail the chronological conclusions of Albright.[7] Plate 3 shows a foundation trench for one of the walls of Saul's Fortress from which came potsherds dating the construction of the fort to the time of Saul.

It should be stressed that conclusions of *stratigraphic* excavators since World War II are trustworthy. Since the scientific standards for obtaining excavation permits have not been very strict in Jordan, many archaeological expeditions even today do not excavate stratigraphically. As a result they produce findings which are not trustworthy, if they publish findings at all. In recent times persons with little or no archaeological background have undertaken such projects as the quest for Sodom and Gomorrah under the Dead Sea,[8] a search for the body of Moses,[9] and a hunt for the treasure mentioned in the Copper Dead Sea Scroll.[10]

Unfortunately, even expeditions sponsored by recognized universities or national archaeological schools at times fall far below currently accepted standards of excavation direction and technique. Such excavations were begun recently at one of the most important early Christian sites in Palestine despite serious misgivings about the excavator's competence on the part of leading Palestinian archaeologists and New Testament scholars. Another recent university excavation in progress approximates the standards of Palestinian excavators at the very beginning of the century: tomb groups were mixed in excavation and recording, and the excavator was warned by colleagues not to publish as contemporary, forms which stratigraphic evidence elsewhere clearly separates by hundreds of years. Obviously, the results of such excavations cannot be trusted.[11]

SURFACE EXPLORATION IN PALESTINE

While we usually think immediately of excavations when archaeology is mentioned, there are really two important branches of archaeological study. The first involves the study of standing monuments and surface remains. This has always been the neglected side of Palestinian archaeology, perhaps more so now than in the past. There has been no worthy successor to H. C. Butler, the master recorder of ancient monuments, who worked in eastern Palestine at the beginning of the century.

Topographical study of surface remains (mostly potsherds and flints) in Palestine is largely associated with the name of Nelson Glueck.[12] Except for his work, very little effort has been put forth in this direction in recent decades. In the past few years the German Institute has begun more intensive topographical work in Jordan, and a thorough surface survey, which will take years to complete, has been begun in Israel. An assessment of this work will be possible when more detailed studies by Siegfried Mittmann and others appear.[13]

What are the contemporary standards by which this work can be judged? The quality of surface archaeological investigation depends upon at least three important factors. The first is the breadth and depth of the topographer's or survey team's background and skills. The second is the amount of time and care taken in on-the-site investigation and recording. Third is the skill with which the material is organized and published. It is obvious that, if there is no person competent as an architect and in the history of architecture, the recording of an ancient surface monument will suffer. It is just as true that if any topographical surface study is made without the services of an archaeologist skilled in the whole range of Palestinian pottery chronology, worthwhile results cannot be expected. No matter how competent the survey, if it is not published, it will never serve a very useful purpose, and a publication is of value when it clearly and accurately presents the evidence gleaned in the survey.

The surveys of Butler and Glueck in most instances consumed an amazingly small amount of time. Where these have been followed up by more detailed work, their conclusions frequently have needed modification. This suggests that the surface side of Palestinian archaeology is still in its infancy. It is undoubtedly true that even today there is a great wealth of important historical material available to the Palestinian archaeologist without moving a spadeful of earth.

ARCHAEOLOGICAL EXCAVATION IN PALESTINE

Staff Competence: Stratigraphy

Basically the same three factors involved in evaluation of surface exploration are important in considering the work of excavators, and we shall consider these factors now in more detail. The first involves the breadth and depth of competence of the excavation team. This competence may be considered in three categories: stratigraphy, typology, and analysis. It is essential in the first place that the earth and its contents be removed layer by layer, reversing the order in which the layers were deposited. This sounds very simple but in practice is exceedingly difficult. Often successive layers of dirt are so similar that they can be separated only by a very experienced hand. Even mudbrick walls are often difficult to separate from the matrix in which they are imbedded. Matters become even more difficult when the stratigraphy is complex and disturbed, as is usually the case. The layer-upon-layer accumulation that forms ancient mounds in the Near East is commonly interrupted by pits, silos, cisterns, robber trenches, clearance operations, erosion channels, foundation trenches, modern construction, and animal holes. Any of these elements which is not isolated can vitiate the interpretation of the archaeological evidence. A pit dug with the layers into which it was cut will contaminate the earlier layers with the later pottery and lead to mistaken chronological conclusions. If, for example, material from the large Arab pit in SW 6-6 on Plate 4 were excavated with the Iron age layers into which it was cut, the Iron age layers would be dated to the Arab period.

It might be well to ask just how much excavation in Palestine is now being undertaken in good stratigraphic tradition. While some stratigraphic excavation was undertaken before World War II, great emphasis has been given to improving methods of excavation by Kathleen M. Kenyon in her excavations at Jericho (1952-58) and Jerusalem (1961-67). The main trenches of these excavations are illustrated in Plates 1 and 6. The methods employed at these sites have a long tradition in British archaeology and may be traced from the days of Augustus Henry Lane Fox Pitt-Rivers (1827-1900). They have been improved and refined by more recent British excavators such as Miss Kenyon and Sir Mortimer Wheeler, but when Americans designate their introduction into Jordan the "Wheeler-Kenyon method,"[14] British colleagues bristle at the superficial way in which a number of Americans have understood and employed the British techniques.

This tradition is ably and actively being employed and developed in Jordan by Kenyon's colleagues and students, notably Peter Parr, Crystal Bennett, Diana Kirkbride, Basil Hennessy, and Kay Wright. Peter Parr's excavations at Petra have unearthed a vast amount of material clarifying the history of the Nabataean capital and its subsequent development under the Romans (Pls. 7 and 8).[15] Crystal Bennett's daring campaigns atop Umm el-Biyara, the rocky massif that dominates Petra, have brought the first shafts of light on the history of the Edomites (Pl. 9).[16] At the Mesolithic–Pre-Pottery Neolithic (8500-500 B.C.) site of Beidha, just north of Petra, Diana Kirkbride has found village upon village of houses more consistently planned than in any previous Palestinian excavation of any period (Pls. 10 and 11).[17] Their connections with contemporary life from Jericho to Anatolia could hardly have been guessed a few years ago. Early in 1967 Basil Hennessy began excavations which gave promise of clarifying the intricate stratigraphic history of Teleilat el-Ghassul, the classical Late Chalcolithic site of the fourth millennium B.C. in the Jordan Valley near the north end of the Dead Sea (Pl. 12).[18] At Tell Ikhtenu, near Ghassul, Kay Wright has come upon the first extensive plans of buildings, albeit quite insubstantial, of the Middle Bronze I period, about 2000 B.C. (Pl. 13).[19]

Americans, Australians, Dutch, Danes, and others have profited from association with Kenyon's excavations. Outstanding among these is Hank Franken, director of the Dutch excavations at Tell Deir 'Alla in the Jordan Valley (Pl. 14), which have been in progress since 1960. In my judgment he is the most careful excavator in Palestine, and it is fortunate that two of the greatest epigraphic finds ever made by a Palestinian archaeologist have been unearthed under his supervision. The first of these was a group of tablets in a hitherto undeciphered script from a massive destruction in the temple precinct (Pl. 15).[20] The other discovery was made in 1967 in a collapsed room of the sixth century B.C. Its frescoed walls had been covered with Aramaic religious texts not yet published.[21] Plate 16 shows the excavator's wife, Ann, a competent archaeologist in her own right, and an assistant treating the fragile frescoes.

Stratigraphic methods have had less direct but still important influence upon French and American excavations. Roland de Vaux, doyen of Palestinian archaeologists, has continued the earlier Palestinian tradition of excavation of Reisner, Fischer, and Albright, but he has judiciously incorporated elements of the British stratigraphic tradition. He is certainly one of the few who stand apart from the generally appalling French tradition of excavation in the Near East.[22] His work has been concentrated on Tell el-Far'ah, biblical Tirzah (Pl. 17), and the Essene monastery at Qumran, where finds have shed light on the community that produced the Dead Sea Scrolls (Pl. 18).

The influence of the newer methods on American archaeology has been sporadic and delayed. It was first felt at Dhiban, a smaller American excavation in Moab, staffed in part with supervisors who had worked at Jericho.[23] The Shechem excavation, begun in 1956 by G. Ernest Wright, attempted to employ the newer methods but fell short of the British tradition (see p. 85 *infra*). The final state of the main excavation area after the 1966 campaign, with squares excavated to various Hellenistic, Iron II, Iron I, and Middle Bronze levels, betrays procedures hardly in keeping with the newer methods.[24]

The Shechem expedition has provided many students with opportunities for field experience, and some of them have gone on to lead excavations. Joseph Callaway competently followed the British tradition in his field at Shechem and in 1964 began a series of campaigns at et-Tell, traditional Ai of the Bible (Pl. 19).[25] William Dever has taken over leadership of the Gezer excavation, begun by G. Ernest Wright in 1965. The combination of British and American methods with American field supervisors and volunteer labor has resulted in a well-organized, careful excavation (Pl. 20).[26]

This represents a fairly complete survey of expeditions which have undertaken careful stratigraphic excavation in Palestine up to 1967. Even in these excavations where the newer techniques are well understood, there is at times much less stratigraphic digging than the excavator desires. The newer methods require a large number of competent field supervisors who are able to keep the detailed records required. Up to now it has been necessary to use foreign supervisors almost exclusively for this recording. It is difficult and expensive to bring a large number of trained supervisors to the Near East, and frequently an excavation staff has a large proportion of inexperienced field supervisors. Some confusion of stratigraphy is almost inevitable before a novice is able to manage his operation stratigraphically.

Further, it is necessary that the workmen doing the actual excavating be able to dig layers of earth separately. This is a skill which takes a long time to acquire; very few local workmen or foreign supervisors have mastered it. There is much competition among excavators in Jordan for these skilled diggers. In Israel the higher cost of labor has led to the practice of conducting excavations with the use of volunteer labor. These volunteers, mostly students from abroad, take the place of hired laborers, usually for shorter periods of time. These volunteers provide a convenient economy as far as they are used in earth removal, but they are frequently used to do the actual digging as well. In the latter instance they are a poor substitute for professional diggers skilled in the separation of layers.

Another consideration suggests caution in utilizing the results of excavations employing the newer techniques. With the exception of two volumes on the Jericho tombs, none of the excavations mentioned above has produced even a first volume of its final excavation report. Some have provided more comprehensive preliminary reports than others, but ordinarily not enough evidence can be included in a preliminary report to make it possible to check the conclusions reported. It is advisable to suspend final judgment about the excavations mentioned until their final reports are in.

There seems to be some truth in the observation that those

archaeologists who do the best work in the field are often those who find it most difficult to set their results down on paper. In some cases the same perfectionism which results in meticulous work in the field causes delay after delay in the effort to produce a perfect publication. In other cases the drive to vigorous outdoor field activity is not matched by the correspondingly necessary drive to sit at a desk to produce a final report. Others despair at the demanding task of controlling the comparative material or dealing with historical implications. A surprising number of excavations among those mentioned, even after a number of seasons in the field, have no budget or schedule for final study and publication of excavation results. Some of these have begun ten, fifteen, or more years ago, and there is no immediate prospect of even the first volume of a final report.

Further, there is no guarantee that the quality of the final report will correspond with the quality of the excavation. If the reader of the final report is unable to revisualize the process of the excavation and locate the finds in three-dimensional focus, it is hard to see what purpose stratigraphic excavation served, beyond the personal satisfaction of those immediately involved. Consequently, all that can be said about the excavations mentioned so far is that their field techniques make the publication of a substantial amount of empirically stratified material possible.

At this point certain excavations not yet mentioned can be given favorable attention. To leave the impression that excavations not employing the newer methods produce nothing reliable would be entirely unfair. The normative work of W. F. Albright in ceramic typology was achieved with the older methods. With extreme care substantial stratified sequences may be obtained by the older methods. Such has been the result in a number of Israeli excavations. As final reports of these excavations begin to appear, the importance of their results becomes increasingly clear.[27] The backlog of unpublished results of this work may be even greater than that from excavations employing the newer techniques.

The most impressive record of prompt, thorough publication is that of Yigael Yadin. The massive final reports of the first two seasons at Hazor and the plate volume of the third and fourth seasons appeared within three years of the conclusion of the excavation in 1958.[28] This, coupled with the large volume on the Nahal Hever Cave of the Letters[29] and a detailed preliminary volume on Masada (Pls. 21 and 22),[30] not to mention major publications of Dead Sea Scrolls and a more popular two-volume work on ancient warfare,[31] constitutes an incredible record of accomplishment. It should be noted that the Hazor project was achieved with a staff which included such recognized scholars as Ruth Amiran, Trude Dothan, and Yohanan Aharoni, who made substantial contributions to the Hazor publication. In any case, excavations using older methods with such a publication record deserve higher marks than those using newer methods but failing to reflect this in prompt, thorough publication.

A more precise distinction between the older and newer methods is long overdue. The difference is as much in degree as in kind. Since the early days of Palestinian archaeology when vast tells like Gezer were substantially "gone through" for important antiquities, there has been a gradually growing concern for greater care, precision, and detailed recording of excavations. This has led to larger and larger scientifically trained staffs and smaller and smaller areas excavated. The newer methods are, in a sense, a culmination of this trend, though culmination is the wrong word from the broader view; undoubtedly, future archaeologists will look upon present techniques as quite primitive and imprecise.

In another sense, however, the new methods involve a rather radical reorientation from the horizontal to the vertical. The older methods were largely oriented to architectural plans with an emphasis on levels. Artifacts were recorded by room in a particular plan with notation about the relation to its floor(s). When excavation of the plan was complete, that stratum was removed and the next finds recorded according to the next coherent architectural phase. If successive, well-preserved architectural phases occurred, the method could be employed with a fair degree of success, but unfortunately such a situation is more often an archaeologist's dream than a reality. One example of an archaeologist's dream is Tell er-Rumeith, biblical Ramoth-gilead, excavated in 1967 (Pl. 23).[32] Ordinarily, though, the method runs into difficulty when a stratum represents a considerable period of time and there are razings, repairs, and reconstructions, when succeeding phases reuse stones of the previous phase and leave it in tatters, when there are gaps between architectural phases with important patterns of erosion and campsite occupation, when excavation is in an area between buildings, and, in general, when stratigraphy is considerably disturbed or complicated.

In these problem situations the new methods with their vertical orientation prove their effectiveness. The new method relies upon the section, the detailed drawing of the vertical face of an excavator's slice of the mound. Because the intricacies of stratigraphy vary frequently, and in order to make it possible to tie each layer and its finds with a vertical section, digging is commonly based on a six-meter grid with excavation in five-meter squares with meter "catwalks" (preserving balks for vertical section drawing) separating the squares. In this way the entire stratigraphy can be carefully recorded, giving a more detailed and complete occupational history of the mound than the series of architectural plans. The major problem with this method is keeping the excavation in phase so that an entire stratum is laid bare and its catwalks removed before the next stratum down is excavated. There has been a tendency, especially among Americans attempting to employ the newer methods, to get boxed in by the catwalks and to permit each square to take an independent course (see p. 74 *supra*). In this case the plans put together from the various squares are often less satisfactory than the plans of the older excavations.

If there has been valid criticism of the newer methods, it has been that some of the gains of the horizontal-oriented methods have been surrendered in the employment of the newer methods, though this is by no means inherent in their use. At Jericho, Kenyon opened some ten "sites" on the tell. These were opened according to a logic in keeping with the objectives of the excavation and in relation to previous excavation and dumping on the site, but it is a fact that no complete plan has been recovered for any of the until-now unique houses of Pre-Pottery Neolithic A and B. It is argued (by hindsight) that in terms of plans it would have been better to open a larger contiguous area. It is impossible to observe Kenyon's practical reaction, for the situation in Jerusalem dictated the opening of a number of smaller "sites."

The excavations of de Vaux at Tell el-Far'ah have not surrendered the concern for plans of substantial areas while at the same time introducing more effective vertical controls (Pl. 17). Although de Vaux has sunk a five-meter square pit adjacent to the excavations at Qumran "to show Miss Kenyon that I too can dig a five-meter square" (he says this with a characteristic gleam in his eye), he has great respect for her methods and has gained their advantages without adopting them rigidly. In somewhat the same perspective, in my own excavations I have tried to exercise as precise horizontal and vertical controls as possible in digging and recording. Daily top plans to complement the section drawings were first required in the first campaign at 'Araq el-Emir in 1961[33] and have since been adopted by a few other expeditions. At Taanach, too, excavation is confined to two main areas, one near the West Building and the other on the south slope (Pl. 24).[34]

What then of the material gathered by the newer methods

compared with that of the old? Generalization skirts the specific problems in the different periods, some of which are much better known than others, but in general the traditional picture of Palestinian archaeology is such that any significant changes in perspective will require material recorded by the precision of the newer methods. Both methods can be expected to add considerable material to the amplification and refinement of traditional views. Both kinds of material can contribute to the expansion of the typological corpora which are the archaeologists' tools, but the refinement of these tools will come substantially from the employment of the newer methods.

Given the few skilled diggers, the large number of inexperienced field supervisors and volunteers, the relatively small number of excavations (mostly recent) which have employed exacting stratigraphic techniques, and the great length of time for final archaeological publications to appear, the student of Palestinian archaeology has an amazingly small base of reliable and normative stratigraphic material. We can only hope that the frantic pace of excavation in Palestine in the last decade will be matched by a flood of precise and accurate, thorough and discerning final excavation reports. Some of the issues involved in such publication are discussed later in the chapter.

Staff Competence: Typology

The success of work on typology and analysis is dependent upon careful stratigraphic work. Without a body of stratified material, it is impossible to develop a viable typology, and the results of typology and analysis cannot ordinarily be related to history with confidence if the material is not from carefully excavated layers of earth. Typology involves the task of classification of the material remains from strata. This includes everything from walls and fortifications and house plans to weapons and seals and jewelry, but of prime importance is the typology of pottery.

From about 5000 B.C. on, nearly every layer of earth on Palestinian mounds contains quantities of potsherds. In fact, most of them contain almost nothing but potsherds. These sherds make it possible to assign dates to the earth layers and thus to link them to history. Ceramic typology is the study of the changes in pots—their ware, decoration, and especially their form—as one proceeds from the earliest to the latest layer on a mound. When correlations are made with similar typologies at other Palestinian mounds, a relative sequence of Palestinian pottery development is established. At times these layers contain evidence for absolute dating—inscriptions, radiocarbon dates, closely dated imports—so that absolute dates may be assigned to certain points in the sequence. At present it is possible to date homogeneous groups of potsherds from much of the biblical period within a century, and at times even more closely.

Accordingly, it is essential not merely that an excavation dig stratigraphically but that it correlate its material with Palestinian typologies, especially pottery. If an excavation staff does not have the capacity to date its material through competent use of ceramic typology, its finds cannot be dated with confidence and thus cannot be linked precisely with historical times and events. If, for example, an excavator has only a vague understanding of ceramic development and assigns a certain major destruction to the Iron I period, it is impossible to decide whether this destruction should be attributed to an Israelite conquest, a Philistine penetration, or an Egyptian raid between 1200 and 900 B.C. A precise knowledge of the ceramic sequence would permit dating to the twelfth, eleventh, or tenth century B.C., or even closer, and make a historical correlation possible.

It should be stressed that this typological background is essential during the course of an excavation. The excavator who studies his pottery day by day as it is excavated is able to detect immediately errors in excavation: a pit that went unobserved, a missed foundation trench, the failure to separate layers of similar character. In short, it is essential that the excavator keep pace with the excavation with a working hypothesis describing his results. This will certainly be refined as more detailed study is possible after the work in the field is finished, but if such has not been done, the hypotheses developed from studying the dead material months or years after the excavation can never approach in quality the hypotheses developed day by day in the field.

The results of those excavations which have not succeeded in digging stratigraphically or are unable to date accurately the material from their layers cannot produce results of significance for history. There is hope, though, that even under these conditions, if the excavation is published fully enough, archaeologists with command of the material may be able to detect what less competent excavators have missed. These reinterpretations take much effort and are sometimes produced decades after the original excavation.

After the field work is finished, no task is more tedious and time-consuming than the arrangement of typologies and the search for parallel artifacts. In fact, it may not be very far from the truth to observe that the reputations of archaeologists are closely related to the number of times they have gone through excavation reports searching for parallels. This is a pedantic process which easily becomes insufferable for an active intelligence. This situation tends to honor pedantry over creative thought. Many sharp minds, attracted by the romance and adventure of archaeology, seem incapable of mastering the complexity of typological detail required to become a first-class archaeologist. There may be hope in the computer.[35] If typological memory can be stored on-call in a computer, the archaeologist will have much more energy left for considering the broader problems of interpretation and historical significance.

Staff Competence: Analysis

The third area in which an excavation requires skill and background is analysis. By this is meant especially those more technical analyses which cannot ordinarily be done in the field in Palestine: radiocarbon dating; ceramic, wood, and metal analyses; testing of soil, grain, and food samples; study of fossils; determinations of bones, teeth, skin, and leather; spectographic analysis; and the like. Most Palestinian excavations are not large enough to afford or justify having experts competent in these areas in the field, and these must often be carried out after excavation, frequently at great cost of time, effort, and money.

This is a field which is rapidly expanding, and entire books and periodicals are appearing to keep the archaeologist abreast of latest developments.[36] Rather isolated from the places of these developments, it is likely that there will be a considerable time lag before many of these new kinds of knowledge offered by analysis will be sought by Palestinian archaeologists. In fact, at present very few excavations assume responsibility for having more than a minimum of relevant materials analyzed. From this perspective alone, it seems certain that archaeologists of the next decades will look upon the present efforts of Palestinian archaeologists as extremely primitive. What is needed is a first-class experimental laboratory for archaeology at a convenient center of higher learning in the Near East.

Field Investigation

The second major element which determines the quality of an excavation is the amount of time and care taken in on-the-site investigation and recording. It is axiomatic that the larger the sampling, the more reliable are the conclusions of any study. Archaeology is no exception. Roughly only 2 per cent of potentially good archaeological sites in Palestine have been touched, and only in rare instances is more than 5 per cent of a site excavated.[37] If we estimate that perhaps half of the material from excavated sites has actually been published and of that perhaps 5 to 10 per cent has a reliable stratigraphic, typological, and analytic base, the amount of trustworthy data available to the historian is an extremely limited sample.

With such limited and uncontrolled sampling, negative conclusions are always dangerous. At one site, for example, we excavated two squares to bedrock, but only subsequently did we find evidence of occupation in the Chalcolithic and Early Bronze periods. Even after excavating a fairly large quarter of the town, we have no clear evidence of what is known, from literary sources, to be one of the town's flourishing periods. Statements like, "There was no Bronze age occupation at this site," "This area was not occupied in the Iron age," and "There was no sedentary occupation in Palestine in Middle Bronze I," must always be accepted with considerable reservation because of the limited sample of evidence upon which they are based.

This means that the more time that can be spent excavating a site, the larger the staff, and the more that is carefully excavated, the more reliable can be the conclusions drawn by the excavator. This statement needs to be taken in the present context of Palestinian archaeology, where budgets are usually quite small, campaigns do not often exceed two to three months, and excavation proceeds very slowly. It should not be taken absolutely. Kenyon rightly stresses that excavation involves destruction of evidence, and some evidence from a mound now under excavation should be left for future generations to dig with their more advanced methods and procedures. It is also true that preparation of a final report of a fairly large excavation for publication is an extremely time-consuming task; it demands considerable time working away from the field in libraries, museums, and laboratories. This means that after a limited period of time in the field and after a certain amount of material has been amassed, it is essential that a pause in excavation be taken to permit adequate time for study and publication.

The quality of investigation and recording is also important. Many important archaeological finds are made by pure chance, and it does seem very often that the more skilled the archaeologist, the poorer his luck. But it is also true that the more pains an excavator takes in investigating his site, its environs, its contours, its surface remains, its standing monuments, its history and traditions, the better and more effective will be his planning in terms of his objectives. Then, as he digs, each new piece of evidence can be fitted into the fund of available evidence. The recording of this new evidence is crucial, because once it is removed, it is gone forever. All that is left are the plans and sections and photographs of what once was there. With some reason archaeology has been called the science of total destruction.

It is just ten years since I had my first archaeological field experience at Shechem. I was given a small notebook and told to write down observations on anything important that was discovered. We drew no plans or sections; that was left to the architect. There was no absolute elevation and no over-all site grid for us to use. Standing around waiting for something important to appear was quite a bore. In my most recent field experience the dig supervisors had little time to be bored. They were required to draw sections of the four vertical faces and daily top plans to accurate scale of the squares they supervised. They recorded and described each layer and other element they dug with its stratigraphic relation. They recorded potsherds and other objects by layer, and they were responsible for examining their potsherds with the dig's ceramic specialist and recording those results basket by basket. All this was in addition to the constant job of seeing that the workmen were digging carefully and stratigraphically. When the material is later reviewed for final publication, obviously a much more detailed, accurate, and reliable report can be expected under the latter circumstances.

Publication

The third critical element which determines the quality of an excavation is the way in which its material is organized and published. Prior to organizing the material for publication is the much neglected problem of organizing a staff for publication. In Palestine as elsewhere an expedition is associated almost exclusively with the name of its director. Qumran is Père de Vaux's excavation; Jericho is Miss Kenyon's. All too often even in larger excavations this has been related to the fact that almost the entire burden of publication (except for technical analyses) has been undertaken personally by the excavation director.

While it is usually true that the excavation leader is the most experienced and qualified to publish, a large excavation publication inevitably suffers if it does not employ a large publication staff, preferably from among the archaeologists who have been on the field staff. This is desirable from the time factor alone. It frequently takes a busy excavator five, ten, and even twenty years to produce a final publication, whereas this time could be considerably reduced if more hands were involved in the task. Early publication is important, for the longer the publication is delayed, the more blurred is the memory of the excavation results. It is of interest to observe that Kathleen Kenyon, who has by far the best publication record of excavators using the newer techniques, spent the summer of 1968 studying material from the mound of Jericho, where excavation was completed in 1958. Only after that could she begin working on the final publication of the Jerusalem excavation.

The organization and presentation of the excavated material in the publication is of crucial importance. The archaeologist is often pressed for several preliminary reports of his campaigns.

Some make a rather long, detailed report on each campaign; others make only short preliminary reports. These reports are largely confined to the excavator's interpretation of the more important findings. The actual evidence from which others can make independent judgments and interpretations is published in the final report. This commonly consists of a number of cumbersome tomes which begin to appear several years after the last excavation campaign is finished. More often than not final publications of Palestinian excavations have been disappointing. Long delays in publication have at times meant that the work was completed by a scholar who had no part in the original excavation or that the excavator finally dispatched the heavy publication burden without much additional work beyond the field because of the press of other duties. This is especially true in America, where Palestinian archaeology is usually an ancillary vocation alongside another professional position.

There is one school of archaeologists which considers that the final report should limit itself to the presentation of the evidence, leaving interpretation to later scholarly enterprise. Such publications are especially disappointing if one is interested in history. Archaeologists who avoid interpretation usually have little interest in history; they are interested in digging and perfecting the methods of archaeology. Present the evidence and leave the interpretation and historical dimension to other specialists! This is the attitude of the educationist whose concern is developing better methods of teaching but who has little interest in the subject matter.

The final publication should organize and present material so that the reader can reconstruct in his own mind, in three-dimensional fashion, what was produced in the excavation. This is a very demanding and partly impossible task. Who can feel a close contact with an excavation with which he has had no personal contact even upon reading the most perceptive and well-presented final excavation report? There are always questions one would like to ask the excavator. In this light it seems to me an essential requirement that the excavator present in the final publication the best interpretation he can of his material, for he has a unique and more complete perspective on his evidence than anyone else can ever hope for. This interpretation, of course, requires a thorough knowledge of the comparative material and historical sources, just as did the developing interpretation of the material in the field as new evidence came in.

There are two levels of interpretation involved. The first is the material, nonliterary level. It involves the interpretations of the architectural finds and objects in relation to comparative material from other sites in Palestine and the Near East and occasionally beyond. What was the material culture at the site in the tenth century B.C., the ninth, the eighth? How did it compare with neighboring sites, with the rest of the sites in Palestine, with neighboring countries of the Near East? Where did the people come from? What is the origin of this kind of house, shrine, or fortification? What was the function of this building, this installation, this artifact? The dire lack of epigraphic evidence in Palestinian digs makes even these questions often very difficult to answer, a stimulating challenge to the excavator with the available evidence at his fingertips.

The second level involves the relationships to literary sources, in Palestine particularly the Bible. Can this stratum be related to a particular biblical period? Is this building referred to in the Bible? Is this the destruction of the mound mentioned in the biblical account? Are these stones some of the sacred stele decried so often by the biblical prophets? Were these utensils used by an Israelite family from the time of David? Hosts of these kinds of questions may be considered by the excavator as he prepares his final publication. Are such interpretations required, and if so to what extent? This hotly debated topic is discussed and illustrated in the next chapter. Suffice it to say here that no archaeologist who is a student of history will wish to avoid considering such questions.

While overgeneralizing, the concern for historical context is more of an American tradition. It is more in the British tradition to affirm archaeology as an independent profession. There is more of a tendency to consider the archaeologist's task finished when he has produced a three-dimensional report on what his mound consisted of before he demolished it. Let the historian take this material and utilize it for his purposes. A supporter of the American tradition could respond that without knowledge of the history of his site and the problems his excavation might solve, it is difficult to see how he can effectively plan and execute his excavation. To forgo any scraps of material from literary sources that might aid in interpretation would seem irresponsible. Certainly, the more the archaeologist understands of the monuments and artifacts he is excavating, the more effectively he will proceed in his digging. Further, it is extremely difficult to interpret archaeological finds, especially in Palestine where written ones have been so rare. Also, as noted above, it is at least as difficult to reproduce everything that has been observed in a dig in the final excavation report. The report can never put the reader in quite as favorable position as the archaeologist in perceiving the finds of the excavation. Accordingly, the archaeologist should be required to have the background necessary to assess the significance of his material for historical problems. On the other hand, the British can retort that their specialization has been the major factor in improving excavation techniques and standards in Palestine.

We have gone full circle in examining the character and limitations of archaeological evidence, and we return to the starting question: Can archaeological discoveries substantiate the historical accuracy of the Bible? On the basis of almost every individual facet of the discussion above, this question should be answered with a resounding "No!" The comparatively few final excavation reports trustworthy by present standards, the uncontrolled and minimal sampling of the evidence, the relatively few archaeologists who have mastered Palestinian typology, the virtual lack of epigraphic evidence, the postulational nature of the relation between material evidence and the written sources, and the very difficulty of excavating a mound layer by layer in the first place—all characterize the evidence from archaeology as being of a hypothetical nature. A best hypothesis to explain the available data is possible, but to call this the truth or to attribute to such evidence the power to authenticate, verify, or prove the accuracy of the Bible is another matter.

It is against the very nature of archaeological evidence to propose that "archaeology confirms the Book of Books." Such a perspective betrays a complete lack of understanding of archaeological evidence and, even worse, a radically wrongheaded comprehension of the biblical sources themselves. The biblical records partake of the same characteristics and limitations as other historical sources. It is not their nature to be true or false. We can develop a best hypothesis in analyzing the biblical sources, but truth is quite something else. The contention that archaeological evidence substantiates the historical truth of the Bible shows a complete misunderstanding of archaeology and of the Bible.

What about the assertion that this purported accuracy of the Bible is a vindication of the Christian faith? To me this displays a complete failure to grasp the nature of the Christian faith. For me the object of the Christian faith is God, or whatever else the Christian atheists might want to call him. The Christians' God, described in the Bible, certainly has a hand in human history, but he remains a God above and beyond the vagaries and developments of history. It is the height of sacrilege to think that archaeologists in their layers of dirt and tatters of walls would have a key to answering the question, "Is the Christian's faith in God true?" It is veritably the idolatry of falling down and worshiping stones—or archaeology. If a Palestinian archaeologist controlled material decisive for determining whether the Christian faith is vindicated for our time, perhaps he should be considered the "God behind God."

St. Paul had the insight that faith is a "gift of God: not of works, lest any man should boast" (Ephesians 2:8–9, AV). If man has vindicated faith in the Christian's God by his archaeological efforts or his rational excursions, he has actually undermined faith, transformed it into something other than a gift. This gift of Christian faith has been accepted by a long procession of believers in times of the New Testament, through the Christian centuries, and even by some living among us today. There is nothing in the archaeological evidence, the historical sources, or contemporary research that can delimit and define this gift or even prove that it exists. There is no objective way to decide whether it is true or false. Only you may or may not know the truth of this gift in your own heart.

If you do not affirm the Christian faith, do not be deceived by the thought that you have no faith. Do not look down upon faith as a vestige of the superstition of ages past. Despite and because of the limitations of archaeology, the imponderables of history, and the incomprehensible elements of modern man, you do affirm a set of values and priorities in your own world—however large or small. You affirm the framework of your world, and you act out of faith in your affirmation. A reporter could not describe something of your life without saying or implying something about the dimensions of your world and how you evaluate its elements. As you live you affirm; as you describe you affirm. Such affirmations of faith are part of the nature of man and the character of history.

"By faith Abraham obeyed the call to go out to a land destined for himself and his heirs, and left home without knowing where he was to go. By faith he settled as an alien in the land promised him, living in tents, as did Isaac and Jacob, who were heirs to the same promise" (Hebrews 11:8–10, NEB). By faith you decided to read this chapter today. "And what is faith? Faith gives assurance to our hopes, and makes us affirm the realities we do not see" (Hebrews 11:1, NEB).

CHAPTER 4

THE SEARCH FOR BIBLICAL CONNECTIONS

SOME scholars consider that the history of the biblical period begins with the patriarchs, about 2000 B.C. For others it does not begin until the Israelite tribes are in Palestine, about 1200 B.C. or later. This fact would seem to underline what has been said about the extreme limitations of archaeological evidence, the great imponderables of the historical sources, and the facets of man himself which remain beyond his grasp. What is the historian to do in the face of such divergent interpretations of his material by competent specialists in the field? Two things seem required. He must adopt an interpretive approach, and he must determine a method for presenting his interpretations.

His interpretive approach will be at some point along a positive-negative continuum. Does he want to emphasize more the vastness of ignorance about what he is writing or the amazing amount of detailed information that is available on the subject? Does he want to emphasize the heterogeneous opinions held by writers on his subject, or does he wish to present a closely argued case for the view he considers most cogent? Does he consider the contributions of archaeology to the historical sources with a basic skepticism, or does he attempt to maximize the links between archaeological results and the historical sources? His position on questions like these determines his basic approach in writing his history. They are the broad general conclusions to his evaluation of his material. As such they are at the same time as much a reflection of his own character as they are of his competence in dealing with the evidence. The approach inevitably reflects his own degree of optimism or pessimism about understanding man, including himself.

It may be more than coincidence that the more negative view that places the beginning of biblical history about 1200 B.C. developed in Germany, when events there were leading to a great disillusionment about man's humanity. The more positive view developed in a more optimistic American climate. Perhaps it may be said that the approach of the times adopts the historian as much as the historian adopts his interpretive approach, but I would prefer to give the final word to the judgment of the individual historian.

With whatever approach, what method is to be used in presenting the historian's interpretation? The basic answer is simple. He must employ the scientific method. He must assemble his material in the form of a hypothesis which best explains his material. Further testing of the hypothesis or new material may indeed necessitate alterations or a completely new formulation.

The method is complicated by the fact that there are two sets of evidence, two sets of hypotheses, and the problem that is the subject of this chapter is the combination or synthesis of these sets of hypotheses. Ideally, it seems to me, the best possible hypotheses dealing with the archaeological and the literary data should each be developed independently. These independent hypotheses may then be used to refine and delimit each other. Finally, out of the refined hypotheses a synthetic historical hypothesis, utilizing all the literary and archaeological data, may emerge. In practice, these steps will often be telescoped, but it is important to keep the steps in mind. Otherwise, it is very easy to fall into the practice of finding convenient biblical interpretations for archaeological data which would not be sustained by critical archaeological hypothesis. This is the way of those who would have archaeology prove the Bible.

These remarks may seem too obvious to belabor, but permit an illustration which may be helpful in clarifying these comments and at the same time show why such remarks are required in matters of biblical interpretation. Two standard treatments of the Dead Sea Scrolls are those of Millar Burrows and Frank M. Cross, Jr.[1] Burrows has written two long books detailing virtually every major hypothesis about the Scrolls published before his books were written. Cross's book is much smaller and attempts to set forth the best hypotheses about the Scrolls with the evidence available to him. Burrows' approach is extremely negative; only rarely does he consider the evidence sufficient to judge between the heterogeneous views of the scholars he quotes. Cross, while very conscious of the limited evidential base, gives as positive an interpretation as a critical evaluation of the evidence permits.

To cite a specific example, Burrows presents at length the various theories of scholars about the identification of the Teacher of Righteousness and the Wicked Priest mentioned in the Scrolls. Cross dismisses most of these theories out of hand because they are excluded by the archaeological and palaeographic evidence. On the basis of literary evidence alone it is possible to consider candidates for the Wicked Priest from several centuries near the end of the pre-Christian era. The evidence from the excavation of Qumran and from the datings of the scripts in which the Scrolls were written specifies the possible time of the Wicked Priest much more closely, and only a very few hypotheses need consideration. Cross espouses one of these as the best interpretation of the evidence presently available. The methods used by Cross would seem to be those that should be used in developing hypotheses about the biblical period based on archaeological and historical sources.

Let us turn, then, to two examples illustrating the problem of combining biblical and archaeological hypotheses.

THE PATRIARCHS

The first problem selected to characterize the difficulties involved in combining biblical literary sources and the evidence of archaeology is that of the patriarchs. Scholars who begin the study of biblical history about 1200 B.C. consider the development of the patriarchal narratives in the context of the tribal confederacy, which developed during the period of the judges. Those who begin their study of biblical history about 2000 B.C. prefer to examine the patriarchal traditions in what they consider their authentic setting in the early second millennium B.C. Both sides consider the patriarchal stories biblical prehistory and agree now that the patriarchs were actual historical people. The heart of the controversy revolves around the question: Do we know enough to link the patriarchs with a specific point in the general history of the ancient world of the Near East known from literary and archaeological sources? In another form it is the question: Can the patriarchs be assigned close absolute dates? If it cannot be decided whether they should be assigned to the twentieth or eighteenth century B.C., for example, their historical context remains enigmatic. This is the search for biblical connections, the quest for links between the biblical sources and the ancient historical world.

The contrast between the two positions is clearly drawn in the two currently popular histories of Israel.[2] After he sketches the biblical world of about 1200 B.C., Martin Noth begins his history of Israel with the tribal league in Palestine, since this is the first appearance of anything that can be identified as Israel. While the patriarchs were historical persons, the biblical stories about them are traditional survivals in the twelve-tribe league, where biblical tradition "was conceived and developed."[3] John Bright provides a sketch of the Near East in the first half of the second millennium B.C., the period in which he thinks the patriarchal traditions belong. It is impossible to trace the origin and developments of the traditions, but they are an authentic representation of the prehistory of the people of Israel and the place where a study of biblical history legitimately begins.

An evaluation of the historical links of the patriarchs is extremely complex, but we present here a summary of the problems in a much oversimplified fashion. The names of persons and places, the genealogies of the Bible, details of patriarchal life, and the literary and archaeological evidence have generally pointed scholars to the first half of the second millennium B.C. as the period in which the patriarchs lived. The first century or so of this period, that is, the twentieth century B.C., is traditionally called the Middle Bronze I period.[4] The rest of the period is called Middle Bronze II with subdivisions IIA, IIB, and IIC, assigned roughly to the eighteenth, seventeenth, and sixteenth centuries B.C. The earlier Middle Bronze I period forms the latter part of an extended period in which there was no urban life in Palestine. This period began with the destruction of Early Bronze urban life during the course of the twenty-third century B.C. and lasted into the nineteenth century B.C.[5] The archaeological evidence for the period consists of campsite and other insubstantial occupation on some of the mounds of Palestine, occupation in caves, and many scattered campsites especially along the desert fringe of eastern and southern Palestine; but by far the greatest amount of evidence comes from a large number of cemeteries scattered throughout Palestine.

Their settlements on mounds and their campsites are usually

represented by tiny scraps. Occasionally some of their material remains are better preserved in caves. The purchase of the Samaria Papyri led to the discovery of one such cave in the hill country of central Palestine about midpoint on a line between Samaria and Jericho. While clearing the cave in which the Bedouin had discovered the papyri,[6] we were attracted by a tiny passage in a neighboring cave called the Cavern of the Sleepy Ones. In this mammoth, labyrinthine cave, which included a seemingly interminable underground stream and a cavern larger than a football stadium, we found the undisturbed remains of Middle Bronze I habitation buried under a thick deposit of bat guano. Besides a few animal bones, tools, and a lamp, the finds consisted of large jars for storing grain and liquid and the first group of intact cooking pots from the period—larger cooking pots than from any other period of Palestine's history. The entrance to the cave and examples of the pots are illustrated in Plates 25 and 26.

In the earlier part of the nonurban period, traditionally called Early Bronze IV, the tombs commonly contained single articulated burials.[7] This means that the bodies were buried before the flesh had decayed. These burials were either under heaps of stones called cairns or in shaft tombs. The latter consist of a shaft cut into soft limestone at the base of which is a small entrance to a chamber, usually dome-shaped, where the body was placed with a group of pots and perhaps a copper weapon.

In the latter part of the period, usually called Middle Bronze I, the same tradition of single (occasionally double and rarely triple) burial persisted, but most of the burials were disarticulated and partial. Though there are articulated, partly articulated, and even secondarily articulated burials, most interments consist of an incomplete heap or scatter of bones. At times the bones were omitted altogether. Grave goods consisted of occasional copper pins and weapons, beads, and mostly pottery. Each group of tombs had its own distinctive features both in plan and in contents. At Jericho, for example, Kenyon distinguished round-shaft tombs, square-shaft tombs, dagger tombs, bead tombs, and others.[8]

While excavating the Cavern of the Sleepy Ones we learned of a nearby Middle Bronze I cemetery at Dhahr Mirzbaneh.[9] The tombs were typical and not very exciting. They had round shafts, some well over two meters deep, and a large boulder blocked the chamber entrance at the base of the shaft. The large dome-shaped chambers, cut into the limestone with considerable effort, contrasted markedly with the careless scatter of disarticulated bones and pots found inside. (For drawings and photographs of a typical tomb see Pls. 27 and 28.) This kind of evidence is generally used to portray Palestine in this period as the theater in which clans of seminomadic pastoralists roamed the country with their flocks. Each group of tombs represents a different clan, and the disarticulated burials are explained by an annual or semiannual return to the clan's cemetery.

The Middle Bronze II period presents a striking contrast with the nonurban phase. Middle Bronze IIA involves the arrival of new people with entirely different settlement patterns and material culture.[10] They rapidly spread their urban civilization southward through Palestine. Most of the campsites and cemeteries of the nonurban folk were abandoned, not to be touched again until they attracted the attention of modern archaeologists. The bearers of the new civilization introduced the multiple burial tradition which had been characteristic of urban life in the Early Bronze age.

These newcomers were followed by the Hyksos, who swept southward through Palestine and took control of Egypt in the seventeenth and sixteenth centuries B.C.[11] Their strongholds were surrounded by steep, plaster-faced embankments crowned by massive ramparts; typical examples have been excavated at Megiddo, Taanach, Shechem, Gezer, Jericho. and many other sites. A section across the western defenses of Taanach, showing several phases of the Hyksos embankment, is illustrated in Plates 20 and 29. Just inside this defense line was the large, well-preserved house, presumably a dwelling of one of the Hyksos rulers of Palestine, shown in Plate 30.

This archaeological evidence from Palestine is not illuminated by related epigraphic finds or literary sources from Palestine apart from the Bible, but there is literary material from Egypt and Mesopotamia which sheds light on the situation in Palestine indicated by the archaeological evidence. In Palestine's earlier nonurban phase, Egyptian texts portray Palestine as a backwater where sand-dwellers lived. Egyptian traders with Syria preferred the sea route to the land route through Palestine, and Egypt's main concern with the sand-dwellers involved measures to prevent or control their entrance into Egypt. When Egyptian adminstration was weakened in the First and Second Intermediate periods, sand-dwellers flocked into Egypt.

The Execration texts make it clear that urban life was being revived in Palestine in the nineteenth century B.C. These texts, inscribed on statuettes or vases, contain the names of rebels against Egyptian authority. By some kind of sympathetic magic the breaking of the figurines or bowls was thought to put these rebels at the mercy of the pharaoh. Two groups of these texts have been dated to near the beginning of the nineteenth century B.C. and later in the century respectively. The later group shows an increase in the number of city-states over tribal units.

The earliest phase of the urban Middle Bronze II period is little known from archaeological remains in Palestine, and its connections with Egypt are still partly obscure. In the later Hyksos phases, there is a wealth of material illustrating intercourse between Egypt and Palestine in pottery, scarabs, alabaster vases, and jewelry. The closely dated Egyptian material provides absolute dates for the Palestinian parallels.

Since the patriarchal stories attribute Amorite personal names to the patriarchs, the literary evidence from Mesopotamia and Syria on Amorites is especially relevant to our problem. The Amorites lived along the fringe of the Syrian desert west of Mesopotamia. At the same time the Egyptians were taking measures to keep out the sand-dwellers, about 2000 B.C., the Mesopotamians were taking similar precautions to keep the Amorites from eroding their borders. The Mesopotamians were even less successful than the Egyptians, for leadership of much of Mesopotamia passed to Amorites, and important city-states developed also in their homeland and westward in Syria.

From one of these city-states, Mari, come hoards of tablets belonging mainly to the eighteenth century B.C., which shed considerable light on the related world of the patriarchal stories.[12] Further light on the legal and traditional practices of patriarchal times comes from the Nuzi tablets. Nuzi is another of the Amorite city-states, and its tablets belong to the fifteenth century B.C.[13] The Mesopotamian origins of the patriarchs described in the Bible seem to find clear support in these documents. The fact that the patriarchal traditions can be clarified by documents from the eighteenth and fifteenth centuries B.C. is an indication of how broad and general are the links between the patriarchs and a precise historical context.

We have, then, the picture presented by Palestinian archaeology and its general historical setting provided by Egyptian and Mesopotamian sources. The indications of Mesopotamian and Amorite origins in the patriarchal sources give a ring of authenticity when set against Mesopotamian evidence. The crucial questions are: When did the patriarchs migrate to Palestine? With what archaeological phase in Palestine are they to be associated? We are searching for biblical connections for the mute evidence from Palestinian archaeology. Should the patriarchs be associated with the campsite occupation and shaft tombs of Middle Bronze I, the restorers of urban life in Middle Bronze II, or even the subsequent Hyksos period? Or were they perhaps a smaller independent movement for which we can expect no archaeological evidence? Or could they perhaps have been associated with both the nonurban and the urban phases?

The traditional view of leading Palestinian archaeologists like Roland de Vaux, Kathleen Kenyon, and Nelson Glueck associates the Middle Bronze I period with the patriarchs. De Vaux's view is that the coming of the Amorites resulted in the destruction of Early Bronze urban life, and their sedentation produced the urban life of Middle Bronze II. Kenyon sees in the disarticulated burials evidence of nomadic life and in the various Middle Bronze I cemeteries indications of its tribal organization. This compares very favorably with the stories of Abraham and Jacob and their clans wandering with their large flocks. W. F. Albright sees in the extensive campsite occupation of Middle Bronze I evidence of trade between Egypt and Mesopotamia along donkey caravan routes.[14] The general conclusion is that the evidence from Middle Bronze I is to be assigned to the Amorites, and Nelson Glueck calls the period the Age of Abraham.

Because of the similar characteristics of the sand-dwellers described in Egyptian texts and the Amorites mentioned in Mesopotamian documents, it is argued that the sand-dwellers should also be considered Amorites. Confirmation of the identification is seen in the names of the Execration texts, which are Amorite.

While this traditional hypothesis relating biblical and historical-archaeological tradition has been widely accepted, it is not without difficulties. Can the Amorites be associated with the long period of nonurban occupation and also with the sudden developments of civilized life at the beginning of Middle Bronze II? Is not quite a new and different population element involved in the new urbanization? What evidence is there for

Mesopotamian connections with Middle Bronze I Palestine? The answer to the last question is that there are no Mesopotamian artifacts and hardly any reminiscences of them in the archaeological evidence from Palestine. Those would be expected if there had been trade routes through Palestine such as Albright postulates for the period. In fact, there are great differences at this time between Palestine and Syria, where urban life persisted in Middle Bronze I. There is even a text which says that the Amorites did not bury their dead.[15] While this record is from an extremely biased context, it could hardly be a description of the folk who spent so much time and effort on their shaft tombs.

Outside Mesopotamia, on the other hand, there are very interesting and attractive parallels to the Middle Bronze I shaft tombs. Parallels to the copper pins and weapons found in the tombs may be traced from Syria to Cyprus, to the southern coast of Turkey, to the Cyclades Islands and the Greek mainland, to Sicily, Sardinia, and western Europe. The same may be said of some of the pottery forms. Parallels to such exotic Palestinian ceramic forms as a cup with a carination near the base, having a pierced lug handle attached to the carination, may be cited from excavations in Sardinia, France, and Switzerland.[16] In contrast, these kinds of parallels tend to disappear as one moves eastward across Syria toward Mesopotamia.

Parallels to the burial practices of Middle Bronze I are found in the same regions as artifact parallels. These include shaft tombs, single burials, articulated and disarticulated inhumations, small cemeteries with individual tribal characteristics. More important, the upheaval which destroyed Early Bronze urban life in Palestine is matched in Syria and Anatolia by very similar developments.[17] The farther east one looks in Syria and the closer one comes to Mesopotamia, the fewer are the traces of this upheaval. It seems to have spread through central Anatolia from the northeast, and the most striking parallels yet found for the pottery of Palestine in Middle Bronze I come from Central Asia in the vicinity of Tashkent and Samarkand.[18]

Central Asia may seem a long way from Palestine and the proposed connections rather incredible. Evidence in their favor is rapidly mounting, especially from the Bab edh-Dhra' cemetery at the edge of the Dead Sea Lisan. This cemetery, excavated in 1965 and 1967, by conservative estimate contains over a million burials and artifacts—by far the largest known in Syria-Palestine.[19] This evidence suggests that the Middle Bronze I shaft-tomb folk were the last in a series of migrations ultimately from the steppes of Central Asia into Palestine, beginning in the latter part of the fourth millennium B.C.[20] Some of them settled the same kind of marginal land they had known in their homeland, land on the desert fringe—barely used before or since in Palestine.

This evidence casts strong doubts on the traditional Amorite identification of the Middle Bronze I shaft-tomb folk of Palestine. The Middle Bronze I remains may belong to an entirely different group of people, hitherto unrecognized in Palestine. In the publication of the Dhahr Mirzbaneh Middle Bronze I cemetery, I have suggested that these may be the biblical Perizzites, for the name connotes dwellers in open country. It would be hard to find a more appropriate designation for folk with the settlement habits of Middle Bronze I. If such an identification is accepted, the coming of the Amorites can be related to the newcomers of the Middle Bronze IIA period, though some Amorites undoubtedly had contacts with shaft-tomb folk before this.

Even if it seems better to postulate that the Amorites are to be related to the new peoples arriving in Palestine beginning in Middle Bronze IIA, the position of the patriarchs remains obscure. Just what connections the various patriarchs had with the Amorite incursions or the subsequent Hyksos movement cannot be more than vaguely postulated on the basis of present evidence. A good indication of this is the summary of W. F. Albright, who has been as positive as any scholar in emphasizing the historicity of the patriarchal traditions:

> The Middle Bronze Age corresponds to the Patriarchal Age of the Bible, though it is not yet possible to date the migration of Abraham from Mesopotamia or of Jacob into Egypt precisely. In the writer's present opinion the Terachid movement from Ur to Harran and westward may have taken place in the twentieth and nineteenth centuries, and Jacob's migration to Egypt may have fallen somewhere in the eighteenth or more likely the seventeenth century, in connexion with the Hyksos movement.[21]

What does this mean for our search for connections between the historical-archaeological and the biblical material concerning the patriarchs? There do seem to be broad general connections between the patriarchal stories and their asserted Mesopotamian background. If the patriarchs were not historical persons, they were certainly described as an authentic part of the world out of which they are purported to come. More than this is hard to say, because no historical or archaeological evidence offers direct links with the patriarchs. If we attempt to link the patriarchs with the archaeological evidence from Palestine, we are in a still more difficult position, for it is not agreed by specialists to which archaeologically defined group of people in Palestine the patriarchs should be assigned.

Under such circumstances it is hardly appropriate to say that the history of the biblical period begins about 2000 B.C. Since it has so far proved impossible to place the events of the patriarchal narratives into a coherent and concise chronological framework, they can hardly be considered historical. There is still an unpenetrated veil between the patriarchal traditions and the historical events which lie behind them. It might be argued that since evidence makes it reasonable to postulate that the patriarchs should be associated with the Amorite movement, their status has been raised to that of a history-bearing group. Further, it might be reasonably proposed that the developments of the Middle Bronze IIA period in Palestine should be attributed to the Amorites and their patriarchal element. Still, since the link between the patriarchs is neither precise nor clear, the movements of the Amorites and patriarchs to Palestine obscure, and the Middle Bronze IIA period little known, to urge such postulations would seem to me to be getting ahead of the evidence.

Does this mean that the historian should ignore the patriarchal narratives in his construction of a history of the biblical period? It is quite legitimate for Martin Noth to utilize the later elements in their formation in developing the history of the period of the tribal league. The character of the sources is such that there are legitimate hopes that stronger historical and archaeological links before this time will be forthcoming. Meanwhile, it is salutary for scholars to sift and resift the evidence, for historians to formulate and reformulate better and better hypotheses to interpret it, and for archaeologists to continue to excavate with a view to producing new material to bring the patriarchs into clearer historical perspective.

This conclusion is in sympathy with both Noth and Bright. Noth is correct in his contention that nothing concrete can be said about the history of Israel before 1200 B.C. He is right in holding that the interpretation of the patriarchal narratives of relevance for the history of Israel should begin with an examination of their selection and formation within Israel's history. His approach in writing a history of Israel is quite defensible. Both Noth and Bright agree that there is a historical stratum underlying the traditions but that this is at present unrecoverable. Bright goes further in sketching the historical context of the first half of the second millennium B.C., to which he assigns the patriarchs, and even earlier periods. This, too, is defensible as providing the background for the history of Israel and especially Israelite religion. Noth has certainly not ignored this material; he has done pioneering work on the Mari documents.[22] The history of Israel does not begin before 1200 B.C., but earlier historical material is of importance for understanding the background and traditions of Israel.

THE CONQUEST

The conquest provides another example of the search for connections between biblical and historical-archaeological material. This concerns an event for which there is a considerable amount of archaeological evidence, a great amount of detailed description in the biblical sources, and volumes of diverse opinions and hypotheses produced by modern scholars.[23] What is commonly called the conquest concerns the events associated with the capture of Palestine by a group of tribes under the leadership of Joshua.

The steps of the conquest include a number of well-known biblical stories. Here we may only sketch them briefly.[24] After leading his followers across the Jordan River, Joshua encamped at Gilgal, where a great circumcision ceremony took place. From there, after marching around the city as prescribed by Yahweh, Joshua captured Jericho and destroyed it utterly. He marched on to Ai, but there he was repulsed until Achan and his secreted booty were destroyed. By a ruse the inhabitants of a strong neighboring city, Gibeon, made a treaty with Joshua, which saved them from destruction. Then Joshua's troops defeated a coalition of five southern kings headed by Adoni-zedek, king of Jerusalem. Joshua followed up this victory by a campaign in southern Palestine and destroyed, according to the sources, Libnah, Lachish, Eglon, Hebron, and Debir. Following this he defeated a coalition of kings from northern Palestine and burned the great city of Hazor.

In one account this campaign has been turned virtually into an account of the capture of the entire land by Joshua, but there are elements in this account and another source which indicate that the conquest of the promised land was far from complete after Joshua's campaigns.[25] This latter perspective has led some scholars to take the view that there was virtually no conquest by Joshua at all.[26] Instead, there was a gradual and peaceful infiltration of the sparsely settled central hill country of Palestine by the Joshua tribes. The actual destructive conquest of Joshua is also dismissed by another hypothesis which considers the arrival of the Joshua tribes a trigger that touched off popular revolts overthrowing the leaders of the Palestinian city-states.[27]

This controversy is carried over into the interpretation of the archaeological evidence. Some would interpret it as clearly indicating a major destructive campaign by Joshua's forces; others would say that such attribution is far from clear in an era of instability, frequent wars, Egyptian campaigns, and the incursions of the Sea Peoples. First, let us look at the state of the controversy about 1958 to put into perspective the rapid strides that are being made in biblical interpretation in light of new archaeological evidence. At that time I reviewed the evidence in a paper which favored a substantial campaign by Joshua but admitted that the evidence was inconclusive.

Archaeological evidence by itself made it quite clear that many sites in Palestine, including some of those mentioned in the account of Joshua's conquest, were destroyed toward the end of the thirteenth century B.C., the approximate time of Joshua's conquest.[28] In some of these sites it was clear that a new kind of occupation followed the destruction, and it was also noted that many new sites with similar occupation sprang up in Palestine during this period. This evidence was cited by some scholars as clear evidence of Joshua's conquest, but others protested that the evidence was not above dispute.

Substantial problems do arise when attempts are made to combine the conquest account with archaeological results at specific sites, especially in the early phases of the conquest account. Evidence of occupation at ancient Jericho ceases a century before the time of Joshua's conquest. Et-Tell, the traditional site of Ai, was unoccupied until just after the conquest (Pl. 19). No substantial Canaanite town at the end of the Late Bronze age has been discovered at Gibeon. The problems are not insurmountable: evidence of conquest occupation may have eroded away at Jericho; Bethel may have been "the ruin" that was Ai of the conquest account, and the Late Bronze town may still be awaiting the excavator's spade at Gibeon. Whatever is made of such explanations, positive evidence corroborating the conquest account is strikingly absent at these sites. On the other hand, the latter part of the account seems to fit well with archaeological findings. Lachish and Hazor, for example, suffered major destructions at the time of Joshua's conquest.

The heart of the controversy has been whether or not it can be demonstrated that there are strata which by their finds are subsequent to the Late Bronze Canaanite occupation but prior to the occupation of the Sea Peoples. The chief evidence cited for this has been silos at Tell Beit Mirsim which came from complex stratigraphic contexts. There were two similar silos from 'Ain Shems, but their stratigraphy was obscure. The very existence of separate ceramic groups which were clearly distinct from and later than the Late Bronze ceramic and which were free of everything resembling Philistine pottery seemed to me to point toward the Joshua conquest, but the evidence was admittedly weak and inconclusive.

Subsequently, new evidence has come to light. A definite stratum of occupation with pottery quite distinct from and inferior to the Late Bronze tradition has been excavated at Hazor. This stratum lies upon a destruction layer which may be attributed to Joshua.[29] Shortly thereafter at Tell Deir 'Alla in the Jordan Valley very similar evidence was unearthed, this time at probably the most carefully excavated site in Palestine to date. Here there was a massive destruction of a large temple complex dated by a cartouche of an Egyptian queen to about 1200 B.C. (Pl. 15). Into the destruction ashes was cut the camplike occupation which may be attributed to the Joshua tribes.[30] Over this poor occupation are layers of occupation with Philistine pottery. Similar evidence may be expected from other excavations currently in progress.

This evidence, coupled with the obvious differences in character of occupation and quality of pottery, makes it very difficult to refute a postulation favorable to a substantial conquest by Joshua. Intercity struggles would scarcely have produced a new culture, and popular revolutions would hardly have led to major destructions of large towns. If the conquest merely amounted to peaceful infiltration, to whom are the destructions and occupations between the end of the Late Bronze age and the arrival of the Sea Peoples to be attributed? The destruction of large and heavily fortified towns like Lachish and Hazor can best be explained by a concerted effort on the part of a sizable body of troops under Joshua. It is possible to attribute these destructions to Egyptian campaigns, Sea Peoples without their characteristic pottery, or internecine struggles, but why promote such postulations in the face of clear statements in the biblical sources that these two sites were destroyed by Joshua?

Taken by itself, the literary evidence also points unmistakably to a substantial campaign by Joshua. It is hard to see how the conquest could be largely an invention of later times. What was preserved was a somewhat idealized account, but it was also an account realistic enough to accept that even with the rapid conquest much pacification of the land was still required. The literary stratification is diverse, but it may best be interpreted as favoring a substantial conquest in a rather short period of time. The archaeological evidence supports the view that the biblical traditions developed from an actual historical conquest under Joshua in the late thirteenth century B.C.

I hope that these illustrations have given you something of a feel for the way historians of the biblical period deal with their sources and with the problems involved in correlating historical and archaeological evidence. In a sense we are dealing with the correlation of literary and archaeological stratigraphy. Mounds, we learned, were built up layer after layer as the site was occupied. The archaeologist's task is to set forth clearly what was discovered from each stratum of occupation. The historian must examine the biblical-literary sources for stratification. Here the situation is more difficult because more than a building up of layers is involved. Older material is not merely covered or surrounded by new, but it is itself often recast and reformed. An archaeologist can be reasonably sure that he has separated his layers, but rarely is there a scholarly consensus that a literary critic has satisfactorily separated the strata of his sources.

If we have carefully separated the pertinent stratified material, there are the problems of assigning absolute dates to the strata so that they may be correlated. This is possible if artifacts from excavations or references in the sources can be linked with absolutely dated material, events, or sources of Near Eastern history. If this cannot be done with confidence, problems such as the historical setting of the patriarchs persist. If this can be done with some precision, as in the case of the conquest, it is possible to construct a viable historical hypothesis.

"The Search for Biblical Connections" is a title that might have been used by a person who was trying to prove the Bible true: every new link between the Bible and historical and archaeological material further supports the authenticity of the Bible.

The examples cited should show beyond question that the historian's search never leads beyond hypothesis and can never lead to the authentication of the truth of the Bible. Still, the title is appropriate from the viewpoint of one involved in archaeological work in the Holy Land. He keeps in close touch with his most important and frequently only literary source. As he digs he frequently asks whether the Bible has some explanation to offer for this find or, conversely, whether this find has something to offer to resolve a biblical enigma. Not infrequently the disciplined combination of biblical and archaeological evidence solves old problems, evokes new hypotheses, and raises fresh problems.

Have you ever asked yourself what you might consider the most exciting community in which to spend your life? In America today I would expect communities like Cape Kennedy to be among the most exciting: many people making little and sometimes great discoveries which are rapidly expanding man's world and his horizons. Though I have never been there, I expect that not infrequently little knots of people get together over coffee or cocktails to exchange their latest discoveries, and sometimes important new ideas emerge from these exchanges.

Something like this went on in Jerusalem, Jordan, where I lived. Jerusalem is a very small town, and biblical scholars, theologians, and archaeologists form a disproportionate element of the population. Whether from archaeological colleagues, other scholars, or other members of the community, came the inevitable greeting: "Any new discoveries?" Exchanging discoveries frequently sent one scurrying to the library to check a new reference or to the typewriter to get down new evidence, a new idea, or a new approach.

What about all this excitement in Jerusalem which, to be quite frank, often seems rather far removed from the problems of the modern world? Perhaps the imponderables of history are no less vast than the dimensions of outer space. Perhaps the discovery of some profound ancient poem is no less edifying than pictures of the back side of the moon. Perhaps the decipherment of an ancient language is as stimulating as programing thought patterns for electric brains. Perhaps writing an ancient history is as profound as writing the latest viable science fiction.

Perhaps the discoveries of Jerusalem are even more important than those of Cape Kennedy. The discoveries at Cape Kennedy are concerned with the expansion of man's world. The discoveries in Jerusalem concern man himself. Perhaps historians have more to contribute to our society than cosmic theoreticians. Perhaps archaeological discoveries in Palestine will enlighten men more than finds from an excavation on the moon. Perhaps it is more important for man to understand himself than to expand his world. Perhaps men need more desperately to understand each other than to discover new creatures out in space. If such should be your conviction, ancient and biblical history and archaeology offer stimulating opportunities to expand your horizons.

Plate 1

Plate 2

Plate 3

Plate 4

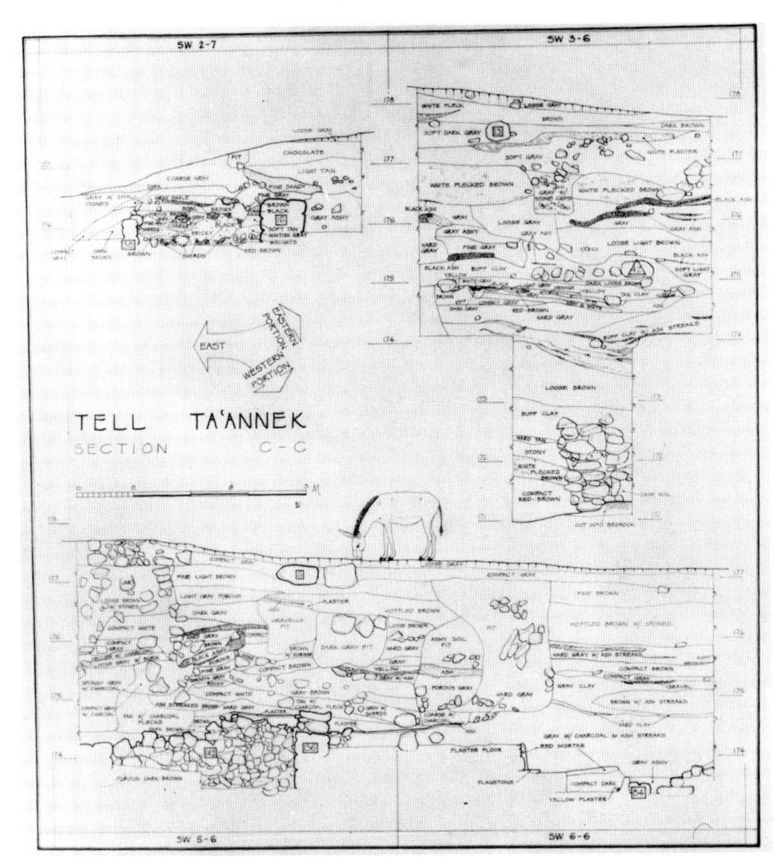

Plate 5

Plate 6

Plate 7

Plate 8

Plate 9

Plate 10

Plate 11

Plate 12

Plate 13

Plate 14

Plate 15

Plate 16

Plate 17

Plate 18

Plate 19

Plate 20

Plate 21

Plate 22

Plate 23

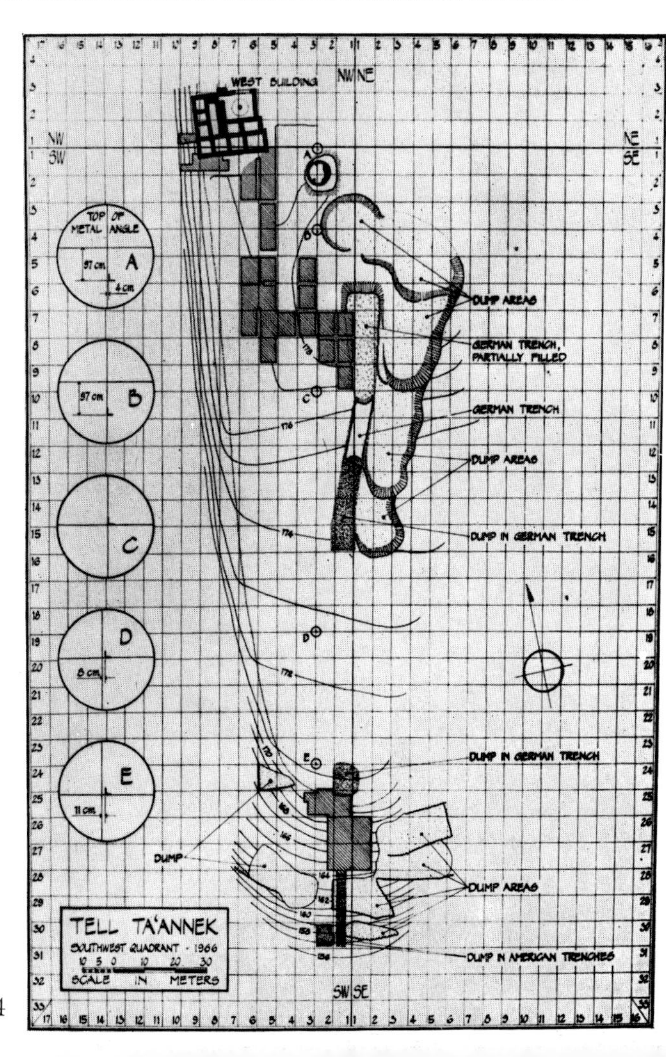

Plate 24

Plate 25

Plate 26

Plate 27

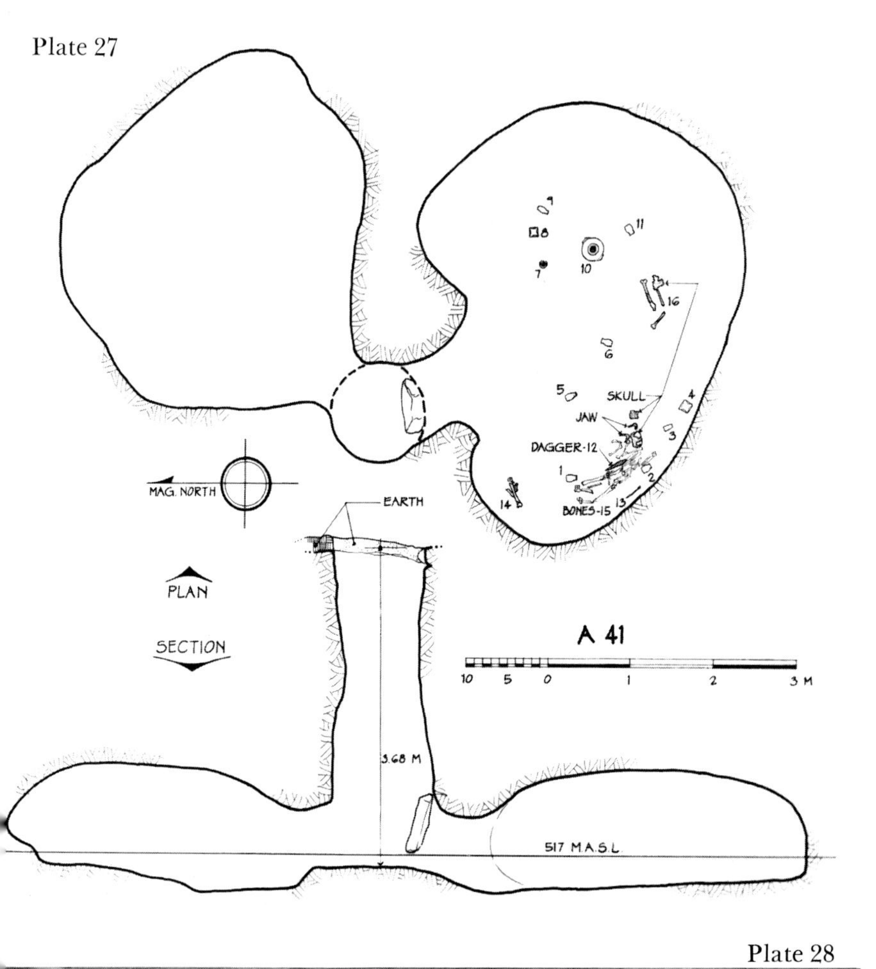

Plate 28

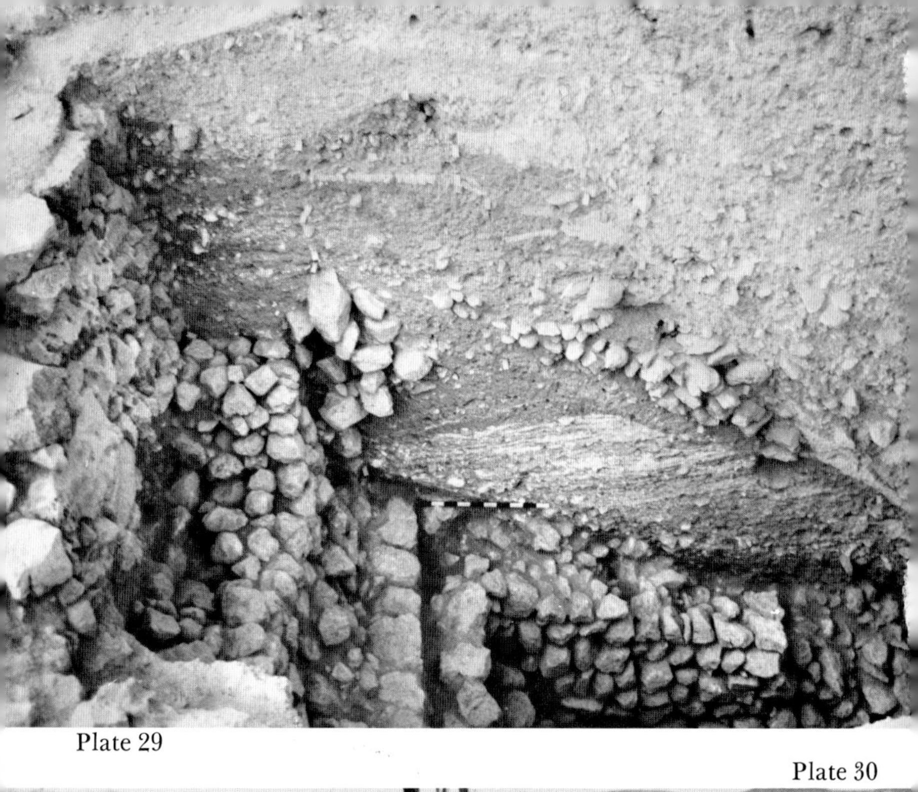

Plate 29

Plate 30

PLATE DESCRIPTIONS

1. Looking south at the north trench of Tell es-Sultan, ancient Jericho. Excavation is revealing portions of houses of the Pre-Pottery Neolithic period. The purpose of the north trench was to locate the Neolithic defense line as a part of the effort to determine the size of the fortified Neolithic town. The Neolithic defense line was located in the vicinity of the foreground of the photograph. The well-preserved mudbrick wall at the back of the trench, set on a stone foundation, belongs to the Early Bronze defense line of the second quarter of the third millennium B.C., illustrating how much larger the Neolithic town was. When John Garstang first exposed the Early Bronze walls, he attributed them to the time of Joshua (13th century B.C.).
2. Looking southwest at the eastern defenses at the crest of Mount Ophel, site of the main trench of the Jerusalem excavations. In the foreground are stairs, which presumably led to the roof of a house destroyed when Nebuchadnezzar captured Jerusalem in 587 B.C. Upon these ruins was built the so-called Tower of David *(left)*, dated by the Kenyon excavations to the second century B.C. To the right is modern consolidation of the steep Ophel slope.
3. Looking south at a tower of the Fortress of Saul at Tell el-Fûl, biblical Gibeah The fairly straight line of the corner of the tower extends upward from near the midpoint of the meter stick, which rests on bedrock. From the top of the small stone projecting at the base of the corner, the line of the foundation trench for the tower may be seen sweeping to the right and up. From the foundation trench the 1964 excavation recovered potsherds, confirming the attribution of the tower to the time of Saul first made by Albright in 1922.

4. Looking south at a section drawing of a balk at Taanach. For location see Plate 24. Upper left excavated to tenth century B.C. floor; upper right to Early Bronze layers on bedrock; lower to level of Late Bronze I building of fifteenth century B.C. Note multiple pits, especially lower right.

5. Looking south at the main trench of the Jerusalem excavations down the east slope of Mount Ophel, site of Old Testament Jerusalem. One end of the water tunnel cut by Hezekiah is near the building by the road in the lower left. A chief purpose of the expedition was to trace the outlines of the city through its history as defined by its defenses. The goal was substantially achieved. The Hellenistic defenses (Pl. 2) are at the summit of the trench, the Bronze and Iron age fortifications (Pl. 6) at the bottom. In the upper left is the village of Silwan.

6. Looking west up the main trench of the Jerusalem excavations on the east slope of Mount Ophel. The man in the left center sits on the Bronze age defenses; the Iron age defenses are behind the man at center. Behind and just right of the balk at the top of the trench the so-called Tower of David (Pl. 2) can barely be seen. The man at the upper left is adding to the dump.

7. Looking northeast from Umm el-Biyara (Pl. 9) across the valley floor of Petra. Beidha (Pls. 10 and 11) is the white area in the upper left. The prominent white line at lower center is the main Nabataean-Roman Colonnaded Street. The white street stops at the Triumphal Arch in the photograph because the street had not yet been cleared beyond that point. Some of the largest funerary façades are hidden in the shadows at upper right.

8. Looking west from just west of the Triumphal Arch of Plate 7 along the recently cleared Colonnaded Street toward the Qasr el-Bint, a well-preserved Nabataean temple, assigned by an inscription found during the street clearance to the time of Nabataean king Aretas IV (8 B.C.-A.D. 40) or earlier. Soundings under the street and in the courtyard of the temple have revealed the earlier history of Petra. At the upper left is Umm el-Biyara (Pl. 9).

9. Atop Umm el-Biyara looking south at excavations of Edomite settlement of the seventh-sixth centuries B.C. Remains consist mainly of walls built up of flagstones *(left foreground)* founded on bedrock. Finds have included the first repertory of Edomite pottery and the first royal seal ever discovered in Palestine.

10. One of the segmented round houses from the earliest stratum at Beidha. Beams were placed in the segment joints, and the rooms

were probably finished to a smooth, round plastered finish. Carbon 14 dates indicate that these houses were built at the beginning of the seventh millennium B.C.

11. Large rectangular house from a later stratum at Beidha, probably postdating the segmented house of Plate 10 by some two centuries. The walls and floor were originally plastered, and there was a central curbed hearth.

12. A typical "square" in the 1967 excavations at Teleilat el-Ghassul. The site has provided the designation "Ghassulian" for a Chalcolithic culture of the middle of the fourth millennium B.C. A fault may be noted in the balk to the left, and a stone-lined pit in the balk to the right. Note the intricate stratigraphy as indicated by the tags.

13. Looking east at Jerusalem-Amman highway crossing Tell Ikhtenu. At the surface, like that seen in the foreground, poor, thin walls of the nonurban phase between the Early and Middle Bronze ages have been located and excavated by Kay Wright.

14. Looking south at the Dutch excavation trench at Tell Deir 'Alla. The visible mound is not entirely built up of layers of occupation; in some places there is only a thin deposit over an outcrop of bedrock. The temple area (Pl. 15) is at the left foreground of the trench. Undeciphered tablets were discovered when excavation was extended to the left of the temple. The room with the Aramaic inscriptions is located almost directly behind the temple area in a southward extension of the trench.

15. Looking west at the massive destruction in the temple area at Tell Deir 'Alla. From this burn a faience vase with the cartouche of the Egyptian queen Tausert, about 1200 B.C., was recovered along with other cultic furnishings. Cut into the destruction layer is campsite occupation which immediately followed the destruction. Above this are layers containing pottery associated with the Philistines.

16. Ann Franken *(left)* and assistant clean and treat the fragile frescoes of collapsed wall fragments from a sixth-century-B.C. room at Tell Deir 'Alla. The frescoes contained long religious texts in Aramaic, an unprecedented epigraphic find in the annals of Palestinian archaeology. In the field an even more delicate process of uncovering and strengthening the frescoes was required before they could be lifted and brought to the registration tent.

17. A section preserved in the excavations at Tell el-Far'ah, biblical Tirzah. The collapsed Early Bronze mudbrick defense wall is

transparent in the balk. Without such clean work, the excavator might easily have removed the wall as a mass of fallen bricky debris.

18. Looking west at the ruins of the Essene monastery at Qumran with the rocky massif of the Dead Sea Scroll caves behind. The Essene cemetery is in the foreground. The Wadi Qumran descends in the rift left of center. The monastic center was founded near the end of the second century B.C. and abandoned at the time the Roman legions swept up to Jerusalem to destroy it in A.D. 70. Virtually the entire monastery has been excavated.

19. Some of the Iron age structures *(back center)* unearthed by the 1964 campaign of the et-Tell Expedition. It was confirmed that there was a small unfortified settlement on the site in the twelfth and eleventh centuries B.C. after a gap in occupation from the Early Bronze age. There is no evidence of late Canaanite occupation at this traditional site of the Ai captured by Joshua.

20. Looking southwest down the southern end of the main trench at Gezer. The wall fragment in the foreground is part of the most massive defense wall yet discovered in Palestine, nearly fifty feet thick. Against it was built a typical Hyksos embankment. The alternating dark and white layers *(center)* are sometimes referred to as the sandwich method of construction; the steep slope line is visible just above them. Behind is a later defense wall which was cut into the Hyksos embankment.

21. Looking east at the massif of Masada, with the Dead Sea, the thin tongue of the Lisan, and the hills of Moab behind. The three levels of Herod's private palace may be noted at the left edge of the massif. Directly below the palace are two somewhat obscure horizontal paths giving access to two levels of mammoth cisterns, the lower line just above the surface of the hills in the foreground. The ascent prepared by Herod may be seen just left of the center of the massif. The only other approach is by the precipitous Snake Path on the western slope.

22. Looking south at a complex of storerooms cleared by the recent Masada excavations. One of the rooms has been left unexcavated to show conditions before excavation. Hundreds of crushed storage jars were recovered from the magazines; some of these are still in process of reconstruction—years after they were unearthed. It can be noted that the operation here was more of a clearance than a stratified excavation.

23. Looking southwest at the East Gate of Tell er-Rumeith, biblical Ramoth-gilead. The 1967 excavation revealed the entrance, behind the shorter meter stick with the gate's door locked still in position

though shattered by destruction fire. The gate is flanked to the left by a guardroom, in which the longer meter stick is placed. Behind the stick is the outer wall of a Solomonic administrative center or fort. Note the floor level of the later stratum atop this wall *(upper left)*, which may be traced in the balk to the floor levels shown upper right. The entire mound was leveled above the destruction of the Syrian stone defenses before subsequent construction and habitation in a planned development project.

24. Plan of the southwest quadrant of Tell Ta'annek, biblical Taanach. Excavation was confined to two areas within the quadrant *(hatched rectangles)*, one south of the West Building, the other at the south slope. All finds are recorded three-dimensionally. When they are recorded by layer, as indicated in the Plate 4 section, they may be located in one of the rectangles of the plan. Each day the supervisor prepares a new top plan of his rectangle, in which important finds are precisely plotted.

25. Looking north at the entrance to the Cavern of the Sleepy Ones in the Wadi ed-Daliyeh. A tiny hole cut by Bedouin at the back led to a labyrinthine cave with miles of passages and caverns larger than football stadiums. Under bat guano were remains of occupation in the twentieth century B.C. and the second century A.D.

26. Cleaning two of the large pots buried under bat guano in the Cavern of the Sleepy Ones. To the left is a large jar, in which was a scum line indicating that it had been used to store liquid. To the right is one of the large, round cooking pots. The jars were used by the pastoral people of Middle Bronze I Palestine in the twentieth century B.C., who often lived in caves.

27. Plan and Section of Shaft Tomb A 41 in the Dhahr Mirzbaneh cemetery. One of the chambers, disturbed and covered with heavy roof fall, was left unexcavated. The other contained the scatter of a few bones representing three individuals, pots, lamps, and a copper dagger and javelin. Contrast the care and effort that went into carving the tomb in bedrock with the careless disposition of the meager contents.

28. View of south chamber of Tomb A 41 looking toward entryway from shaft upper right. Note the careless disposition of the pots and the few long bones of one of the individuals interred at the left. The heap of bones belonging to the main burial are barely visible behind the longer meter stick.

29. Looking south at a section through the defenses on the western slope of Taanach. Note the thick Hyksos embankment at the upper right. Fragments of earlier embankments may be noted beneath it. Below are elements of the massive stone scree defenses

of the Early Bronze age. At the far left is the outer wall of a large Hyksos residence, against which, it may be presumed, the latest embankment originally lay. This is the West Building of Plate 24 illustrated on Plate 30.

30. Looking northeast at the West Building discovered by the German excavations at Taanach. The man at the left stands by the mouth of a large cistern in its great court, the man at the right in the hall from which a stairway led to the second story. The building may be presumed to be a residence of one of the Hyksos feudal rulers of Taanach.

NOTES

CHAPTER I. THE SOURCES OF HISTORY

1. Herculaneum is brought to life in the recent book of Joseph Jay Deiss, *Herculaneum: Italy's Buried Treasure* (New York: Thomas Y. Crowell, 1966).
2. This distinction as well as the illustration of the preceding paragraph reflect the approach of Krister Stendahl. See, for example, his "Biblical Theology, Contemporary," in *Interpreter's Dictionary of the Bible* (Nashville, Tenn.: Abingdon Press, 1962), I, pp. 418-32; "Method in the Study of Biblical Theology," in J. Philip Hyatt (ed.), *The Bible in Modern Scholarship* (Nashville, Tenn.: Abingdon Press, 1965), pp. 196-209; *The Bible and the Role of Women* (Philadelphia: Fortress Press, 1966), pp. 10-24.
3. See Roland de Vaux, *L'archéologie et les manuscrits de la Mer Morte* (London: Oxford University Press, 1961). For a recent summary of the Nag Hammadi material see A. K. Helmbold, *The Nag Hammadi Gnostic Texts and the Bible* (Grand Rapids, Mich.: Baker Book House, 1967). A campaign at the Hamra Dom cemetery near Nag Hammadi by Pittsburgh Theological Seminary in cooperation with the Institute for Antiquity and Christianity and the American Research Center in Egypt has been proposed for December, 1969.
4. On the reconstruction of Solomon's temple see Paul L. Garber, "Reconstructing Solomon's Temple," *Biblical Archaeologist*, 14 (1951), pp. 2-24; G. Ernest Wright, "The Stevens' Reconstruction

of the Solomonic Temple," *Biblical Archaeologist*, 18 (1955), pp. 41-44.

5. The announcement of the discovery was made by Yigael Yadin to the 25th Archaeological Convention of the Israel Exploration Society on October 21, 1967. See Y. Yadin, "The Temple Scroll," *Biblical Archaeologist*, 30 (1967), pp. 135-39.
6. Freya Stark, *Rome on the Euphrates* (London: John Murray, 1966), p. 28.
7. Paul Tillich, *Systematic Theology*, III (Chicago: University of Chicago Press, 1963), pp. 308-13.
8. Cf. Charles A. Beard, "Written History as an Act of Faith," in Hans Meyerhof (ed.), *The Philosophy of History in Our Time* (Garden City, N.Y.: Doubleday Anchor Books, 1959), pp. 140-51.

Chapter 2. The Bible and History

1. For a current attempt to link the flood tradition of the ancient Near East with history see S. N. Kramer, "Reflections on the Mesopotamian Flood: The Cuneiform Data New and Old," *Expedition*, 9 (1967), pp. 12-18.
2. Patrick W. Skehan, "The Biblical Scrolls from Qumran and the Text of the Old Testament," *Biblical Archaeologist*, 28 (1965), pp. 87-100. Cf. Frank M. Cross, Jr., "Aspects of Samaritan and Jewish History in Late Persian and Hellenistic Times," *Harvard Theological Review*, 59 (1966), pp. 201-11.
3. The word "interpretation" might be substituted for "understanding," but the latter has been preferred to connote a more personal affirmation. The former is used, for example, by John Hick, *Faith and Knowledge* (Ithaca, N.Y.: Cornell University Press, 1966), p. 215.
4. Rudolf Bultmann, *Theology of the New Testament*, II (New York: Charles Scribner's Sons, 1955), p. 66.
5. *Ibid.*, pp. 67-68.
6. Paul Tillich, *Dynamics of Faith* (New York: Harper & Row, 1957), p. 88.
7. For a recent summary of his views see Schubert M. Ogden, *The Reality of God and Other Essays* (New York: Harper & Row, 1966). Cf. Robert Funk, *Language, Hermeneutic, and Word of God* (New York: Harper & Row, 1966), pp. 87-108.
8. Cf. Funk, *Language, Hermeneutic, and Word of God*, p. 103.
9. Thomas J. J. Altizer, "Word and History," in *Radical Theology and the Death of God* (Indianapolis: Bobbs-Merrill, 1966), p. 125.

10. Altizer, "America and the Future of Theology," in *Radical Theology and the Death of God*, p. 19.
11. Altizer, in *Radical Theology and the Death of God*, p. 122.
12. *Ibid.*, p. 125.
13. William Hamilton, "The Death of God Theologies Today," in *Radical Theology and the Death of God*, p. 49.
14. Altizer, in *Radical Theology and the Death of God*, p. 133.
15. James M. Robinson, *A New Quest of the Historical Jesus* (Naperville, Ill.: Allenson, 1959), p. 44. See also Ernst Fuchs, "Must One Believe in Jesus if He Wants to Believe in God?" *Journal for Theology and the Church*, I (1965), pp. 147-68.
16. Van Austin Harvey, *The Historian and the Believer* (New York: Macmillan, 1966), p. 175.
17. Cf. the terminology of Altizer, in *Radical Theology and the Death of God*, p. 136.
18. This exposition depends heavily on Harvey, *The Historian and the Believer*, pp. 170ff.
19. Robinson, *A New Quest of the Historical Jesus*, p. 68.
20. Stendahl, *The Bible and the Role of Women*, p. 17. Cf. R. G. Collingwood, *The Idea of History* (Oxford: Oxford University Press, 1946), pp. 282-83, 317–18. For a recent treatment of some of Collingwood's concerns, see Robert Stover, *The Nature of Historical Thinking* (Chapel Hill: University of North Carolina Press, 1967).
21. Altizer, in *Radical Theology and the Death of God*, p. 136.
22. Harvey, *The Historian and the Believer*, p. 171.
23. Hamilton, in *Radical Theology and the Death of God*, pp. 46-50.
24. *Ibid*, p. 40.
25. Cf. Funk, *Language, Hermeneutic, and Word of God*, pp. 37-46.
26. Mircea Eliade, *Cosmos and History: The Myth of the Eternal Return* (New York: Harper & Row, 1959), p. 3.
27. Cf. G. Ernest Wright, "Old Testament Scholarship in Prospect," *Journal of Bible and Religion*, 28 (1960), p. 189. The views of G. Ernest Wright are taken as representative of the biblical theology approach in this section. This approach is less vulnerable to the strictures of James Barr against verbal and linguistic derivation of biblical theology. Cf. *Biblical Words for Time* (Naperville, Ill.: Allenson, 1962), pp. 153–62. The claims of uniqueness for the Bible's theological perspective in the ancient Near East are much more vulnerable. Cf. Bertil Albrektson, *History and the Gods* (Lund: Gleerup, 1967). Another useful critique is James Barr, "Revelation through History in the Old Testament and in Modern Theology," *Interpretation*, 17 (1963), pp. 193-205.
28. G. Ernest Wright, *God Who Acts* (London: SCM Press, 1952), p.

107. On the role of worship and cult as a bridge from past to present see Martin Noth, "The Re-Presentation of the Old Testament in Proclamation," in C. Westerman (ed.), *Essays on Old Testament Hermeneutics* (Richmond, Va.: John Knox Press, 1965), pp. 76-88.

29. Wright, *God Who Acts*, p. 107.
30. G. Ernest Wright, "Archaeology, History, and Theology," *Harvard Divinity Bulletin*, 28 (April, 1964), p. 89.
31. Cf. the approach of Frank M. Cross, Jr., in "The Divine Warrior in Israel's Early Cult," in Alexander Altmann (ed.), *Bible Motifs: Origins and Transformations* (Cambridge, Mass.: Harvard University Press, 1966), pp. 11-30.
32. Hamilton, in *Radical Theology and the Death of God*, p. 28.
33. Martin Noth, *The History of Israel* (English translation of 2nd German edition by Stanley Godman; New York: Harper & Row, 1958). John Bright, *A History of Israel* (Philadelphia: Westminster Press, 1959).
34. Collingwood, *The Idea of History*, pp. 153-54, 202-3, 305, *et passim.*

Chapter 3. The Bible and Archaeology

1. See James Mellaart, *Earliest Civilizations of the Near East* (London: Thames & Hudson, 1965).
2. Paul W. Lapp, "Bâb edh-Dhrâʿ Tomb A 76 and Early Bronze I Palestine," *Bulletin of the American Schools of Oriental Research*, 189 (February, 1968), pp. 12–41. Cf. my "Palestine in the Early Bronze Age" in the *Festschrift* for Nelson Glueck being published by Doubleday.
3. Frank M. Cross, Jr., "The Discovery of the Samaria Papyri," *Biblical Archaeologist*, 26 (1963), pp. 110-21.
4. Kathleen Kenyon, *Digging Up Jericho* (London: Ernest Benn, 1957), p. 262. On her digging methods see *Beginning in Archaeology* (New York: Frederick A. Praeger, 1962), pp. 68-114.
5. Kathleen Kenyon, "Excavations in Jerusalem," *Biblical Archaeologist*, 27 (1964), pp. 37-38. For a more recent summary of the Jerusalem excavations see her *Jerusalem, Excavating 3000 Years of History* (New York: McGraw-Hill, 1967).
6. The material is found in the final report of the Tell Beit Mirsim excavations in the *Annual of the American Schools of Oriental Research*, 12, 13, 17, 21-22 (1932-43).
7. Paul W. Lapp, "Tell el-Fûl," *Biblical Archaeologist*, 28 (1965), pp. 2-10.

8. Ralph E. Baney, *Search for Sodom and Gomorrah* (Kansas City: Cam Press, 1962).
9. Ivar Lissner, "The Tomb of Moses Is Still Undiscovered," *Biblical Archaeologist*, 26 (1963), pp. 106-8.
10. John Allegro's negative results have not been scientifically published.
11. Except for experienced archaeologists who systematically visit other excavations, it is often virtually impossible to assess the reliability of excavation reports. It is something of a paradox that highly critical reviews of excavation reports are most often written by persons incompetent in field archaeology, while archaeologists are more polite than critical in reviews of works of their less effective colleagues. For a refreshing exception see Roland de Vaux's review of J. B. Pritchard's *Winery, Defenses, and Soundings at Gibeon* (Philadelphia: University Museum, 1964), in *Revue Biblique*, 73 (1966), pp. 130-35.
12. See, for example, Nelson Glueck, "The Negev," *Biblical Archaeologist*, 22 (1959), pp. 82-97. Cf. G. Ernest Wright, "The Achievement of Nelson Glueck," *Biblical Archaeologist*, 22 (1959), pp. 98-100.
13. See provisionally Mittmann's unpublished dissertation *Beiträge zur Siedlungs- und Territorialgeschichte des nördlichen Ostjordanlandes* (Tübingen, 1966).
14. Cf. W. F. Albright, *The Archaeology of Palestine* (Baltimore: Penguin Books, 1960), p. 21.
15. P. J. Parr, "Excavations at Petra, 1958-59," *Palestine Exploration Quarterly* (1960), pp. 124-35. Subsequent campaigns have not been reported in detail.
16. Crystal M. Bennett, "Fouilles d'Umm el-Biyara," *Revue Biblique*, 73 (1966), pp. 372-403.
17. Her most recent report is "Beidha 1965: An Interim Report," *Palestine Exploration Quarterly* (1967), pp. 5-13.
18. Unpublished.
19. Unpublished.
20. H. J. Franken, "Clay Tablets from Deir 'Alla, Jordan," *Vetus Testamentum*, 14 (1964), pp. 377–79. A. van den Branden, "Essai de déchiffrement des inscriptions de Deir 'Alla," ibid., 15 (1965), pp. 129-50. Franken, "A note on how the Deir 'Alla tablets were written," ibid., pp. 150-52. Van den Branden, "Comment lire les textes de Deir 'Alla?," ibid., pp. 532-35. Franken, "A reply," ibid., pp. 535-36.
21. H. J. Franken, "Texts from the Persian Period from Tell Deir 'Allā," *Vetus Testamentum*, 17 (1967), pp. 480–81. Cf. J. Naveh, "The

Date of the Deir 'Allā Inscription in Aramaic Script," *Israel Exploration Journal*, 17 (1967), pp. 256-58.

22. Kathleen Kenyon, for example, observes on the French excavations at Byblos that "Byblos was excavated in a series of rigidly horizontal spits (levees) of 20 centimetres. The true stratification was neither published nor observed, and the objects are published purely by spit and location, with no regard for the admittedly irregular contours of the site." "Syria and Palestine *c.* 2160-1780 B.C.," in *Cambridge Ancient History*, I (rev. ed.; Cambridge: Cambridge University Press, 1965), p. 54.
23. The first campaign at Dibon in 1950-51 failed to find significant stratified deposits. Improved methods were employed in the 1952 campaign, but still the pottery of Iron II is published as a group. Improved precision is to be expected from the subsequent work of William Morton, not yet published. Fred V. Winnett and William L. Reed, "The Excavations at Dibon (Dhībân) in Moab," *Annual of the American Schools of Oriental Research*, 36-37 (1964), pp. 24, 55.
24. Until a report on the 1966 campaign appears, see the report on the penultimate campaign in Field VII, "The Fifth Campaign at Balâtah (Shechem)," *Bulletin of the American Schools of Oriental Research*, 180 (December, 1965), pp. 17-26. For a summary of the earlier campaigns at Shechem see G. Ernest Wright, *Shechem: The Biography of a Biblical City* (New York: McGraw-Hill, 1965).
25. Joseph A. Callaway, "The 1964 'Ai (et-Tell) Excavations," *Bulletin of the American Schools of Oriental Research*, 178 (April, 1965), pp. 13-40.
26. William G. Dever, "Excavations at Gezer," *Biblical Archaeologist*, 30 (1967), pp. 47-62.
27. Note, for example, the important ceramic groups from Stratum V at en-Gedi and from Locus 2001 at Ashdod. B. Mazar, T. Dothan, I. Dunayevsky, "En-Gedi: The First and Second Seasons of Excavations, 1961-62," *'Atiqot*, 5 (1966). M. Dothan and D. N. Freedman, "Ashdod I: The First Season of Excavations, 1962," *'Atiqot*, 7 (1967).
28. Yigael Yadin, *et al.*, *Hazor I–III-IV Plates* (Jerusalem: Magnes Press, 1958-61).
29. Yigael Yadin, *The Finds from the Bar Kokhba Period in the Cave of Letters* (Jerusalem: Israel Exploration Society, 1963).
30. Yigael Yadin, *Masada: Herod's Fortress and the Zealots' Last Stand* (New York: Random House, 1966).
31. Yigael Yadin, *The Art of Warfare in Biblical Lands* (New York: McGraw-Hill, 1963).

32. Paul W. Lapp, "Tell er-Rumeith," in "Chronique Archéologique," *Revue Biblique,* 75 (1968), pp. 86ff.
33. On the excavations at 'Araq el-Emir see Paul W. Lapp, "Soundings at 'Arâq el-Emîr (Jordan)," *Bulletin of the American Schools of Oriental Research,* 165 (February, 1962), pp. 16-34; "The Second and Third Campaigns at 'Arâq el-Emîr," *Bulletin of the American Schools of Oriental Research,* 171 (October, 1963), pp. 8-39.
34. Paul W. Lapp, "Taanach by the Waters of Megiddo," *Biblical Archaeologist,* 30 (1967), pp. 2-27.
35. For a pioneering attempt see J. Christophe and J. Deshayes, *Indexe de l'outillage: outils en métal de l'âge du bronze, des Balkans à l'Indus* (Paris: Geuthner, 1964).
36. Some of the recent literature is conveniently summarized by Henry O. Thompson, "Science and Archaeology," *Biblical Archaeologist,* 29 (1966), pp. 114-25.
37. Despite the fact that Palestine is archaeologically one of the best-known countries in the world, its archaeological treasures have barely been tapped. Cf. Paul W. Lapp, "Palestine: Known but Mostly Unknown," *Biblical Archaeologist,* 26 (1963), pp. 121-34.

Chapter 4. The Search for Biblical Connections

1. Millar Burrows, *The Dead Sea Scrolls* (New York: Viking Press, 1955); *More Light on the Dead Sea Scrolls* (New York: Viking Press, 1958). Frank M. Cross, Jr., *The Ancient Library of Qumran and Modern Biblical Studies* (New York: Doubleday, 1958). The last comprised the Haskell Lectures for 1957. G. R. Driver could have been similarly matched with Père R. de Vaux. Cf. especially de Vaux's remarks on the relative importance of literary and archaeological evidence in "The Judaean Scrolls. 2. Essenes or Zealots?" *New Testament Studies,* 13 (October, 1966), pp. 97-98.
2. John Bright, *A History of Israel* (Philadelphia: Westminster Press, 1959); Martin Noth, *The History of Israel,* trans. Stanley Godman (New York: Harper & Row, 1958).
3. Noth, *The History of Israel,* p. 120.
4. Kathleen Kenyon calls the period Intermediate Early Bronze–Middle Bronze, and considers traditional Middle Bronze IIA as Middle Bronze I. This discussion is taken largely from my much more extended discussion of the period in *The Dhahr Mirzbaneh Tombs* (New Haven, Conn.: American Schools of Oriental Research, 1966), pp. 89-116.

5. This is in substantial agreement with the latest published views of W. F. Albright, "Remarks on the Chronology of Early Bronze IV–Middle Bronze IIA in Phoenicia and Syria-Palestine," *Bulletin of the American Schools of Oriental Research*, 184 (December, 1966), pp. 26-35.
6. Paul W. Lapp, "The Samaria Papyri," *Archaeology*, 16 (1963), pp. 204-6.
7. Lapp, *The Dhahr Mirzbaneh Tombs*, pp. 99-100.
8. Kenyon, *Digging Up Jericho*, pp. 186-209.
9. Lapp, *The Dhahr Mirzbaneh Tombs*, pp. 1-4.
10. Roland de Vaux diverges from this view, considering the nomads Amorites and the urban life the result of their sedentation. "Les patriarches hébreux et l'histoire," *Revue Biblique*, 72 (1965), pp. 5-28.
11. The term "Hyksos" is retained in specific disagreement with the pontificating conclusions of the latest work on the subject, John van Seters, *The Hyksos, A New Investigation* (New Haven, Conn.: Yale University Press, 1966). As Hans Goedicke points out in his review *(American Journal of Archaeology*, 71 [1967], pp. 412-13), the views expressed hardly constitute a "new investigation."
12. A recent summary of the extensive literature on the Mari documents is found in Herbert B. Huffmon, *Amorite Personal Names in the Mari Texts* (Baltimore: Johns Hopkins Press, 1965), pp. 1-12.
13. C. H. Gordon, "Biblical Customs and the Nuzi Tablets," *Biblical Archaeologist*, 3 (1940), pp. 1-12.
14. W. F. Albright, "Abram the Hebrew: A New Archaeological Interpretation," *Bulletin of the American Schools of Oriental Research*, 163 (October, 1961), pp. 36-54. Cf. Albright, *Bulletin of the American Schools of Oriental Research*, 184, pp. 34-35.
15. Cf. Lapp, *The Dhahr Mirzbaneh Tombs*, pp. 113-14.
16. *Ibid.*, p. 101.
17. *Ibid.*, pp. 89-91, 104-5.
18. *Ibid.*, pp. 111-12.
19. Paul W. Lapp, "The Cemetery at Bab edh-Dhra, Jordan," *Archaeology*, 19 (1966), pp. 104-111.
20. Cf. chap. 3, n. 2.
21. Albright, *Archaeology of Palestine*, p. 83.
22. For references see Huffmon, *Amorite Personal Names in the Mari Texts*, p. 11.
23. The material is described and annotated in greater detail in my "The Conquest of Palestine in the Light of Archaeology," *Concordia Theological Monthly*, 38 (1967), pp. 283-300.
24. See Joshua 6-11.
25. A convenient nontechnical summary of the literary problems is

provided by G. Ernest Wright, *Biblical Archaeology* (Philadelphia: Westminster Press, 1957), pp. 69-70.

26. Cf. Noth, *History of Israel*, p. 82.
27. G. E. Mendenhall, "The Hebrew Conquest of Palestine," *Biblical Archaeologist*, 25 (1962), p. 73. Cf. the mediating position of Frank M. Cross, Jr., *Biblical Motifs*, p. 16, n. 13.
28. This date is accepted by a consensus of specialists in the field. Cf. K. A. Kitchen, *Ancient Orient and Old Testament* (Chicago: Inter-Varsity Press, 1966), pp. 57-75; John Bright, *A History of Israel*, pp. 112-13.
29. Yigael Yadin, "The Fourth Season of Excavation at Hazor," *Biblical Archaeologist*, 22 (1959), pp. 13-14.
30. H. J. Franken, "Excavations at Deir 'Alla, Season 1964," *Vetus Testamentum*, 14 (1964), pp. 418-19. Cf. *Vetus Testamentum*, 11 (1961), Pl. 5; 12 (1962), pp. 464-69; 14 (1964), p. 219.